W9-AHA-637

Is Tax Amnesty a Good Tax Policy?

Is Tax Amnesty a Good Tax Policy?

Evidence from State Tax Amnesty Programs in the United States

Hari S. Luitel

LEXINGTON BOOKS
Lanham • Boulder • New York • London

Published by Lexington Books
An imprint of The Rowman & Littlefield Publishing Group, Inc.
4501 Forbes Boulevard, Suite 200, Lanham, Maryland 20706
www.rowman.com

16 Carlisle Street, London W1D 3BT, United Kingdom

British Library Cataloguing in Publication Information Available

Library of Congress Cataloging-in-Publication Data
Luitel, Hari S., 1965- author.
  Is tax amnesty a good tax policy? : evidence from state tax amnesty
programs in the United States / Hari S. Luitel.
      pages cm
  Includes bibliographical references and index.
  ISBN 978-1-4985-0008-1 (cloth : alk. paper) — ISBN 978-1-4985-
0009-8 (electronic) 1. Tax amnesty--United States. I. Title.
  KF6334.L85 2014
  336.24'16—dc23

                                                              2014020488

Printed in the United States of America

TO NAINA, WHOSE ARRIVAL IN 2012
BROUGHT NEW MEANING IN LIFE

Contents

Tables

Figures

Abbreviations Used

2SIV	Two Stage Instrumental Variable
cumhaz	Cumulative Hazard
FTA	Federation of Tax Administrators
GDP	Gross Domestic Product
GLS	Generalized Least Square
iid	independently and identically distributed
IRS	Internal Revenue Services
JCT	Joint Committee on Taxation
NASBO	National Association of State Budget Officers
OLS	Ordinary Least Square
US	United States of America
USD	United States Dollar
VAT	Value Added Tax
VDA	Voluntary Disclosure Agreement

Preface

This book is based on my Ph.D. dissertation. In empirical economic research, modeling endogeneity is an important aspect of a research design. Endogeneity refers to the conceptual possibility that the regressors are correlated with the error term. My dissertation departed from incorporating endogeneity in the descriptive research design and was completed in 2005 after I was able to convince a panel of experts on the dissertation committee that in the absence of statistical endogeneity in the data, the sample statistics obtained from a single equation method are best, linear, unbiased estimators (BLUE) of the population parameters. Based on this premise, my first research article entitled, "The Revenue Impact of Repeated Tax Amnesties," written jointly with Russell S. Sobel, was published in *Public Budgeting and Finance* (Fall 2007, Volume 27, Issue 3, pages 19–38).

Despite the publication of the first research article, I was not completely satisfied with my research design because it had not adequately addressed the inherent nature of the endogeneity problem. In my subsequent research, therefore, I was curious to look at state tax amnesty programs from an opposite angle. My curiosity was triggered by the fact that, although not unimportant in absolute terms, the US state tax amnesty collections were small relative to total tax collections. For example, between 1982 and 2012, US state tax amnesties generated an average of only 0.74 percent, and did not even account for more than 3 percent of US state total tax collections.

These short-run revenue gains were, however, accompanied by long-run future tax losses to the states attributable to the amnesty. I was therefore interested in critically evaluating what motivated states to tap into these short-run revenue gains on a repeated basis. The issue has been addressed in "A Reexamination of State Fiscal Health and Amnesty Enactment," written jointly with Mehmet S. Tosun. This paper is forthcoming in *International Tax and Public Finance.*

I moved to Canada in 2010. At that time, I had answers to my research questions and I did not intend to write a book. But several recent developments in US politics have changed my mind. Particularly, the US government shutdown of 2013 not only has revealed the need to rethink fundamentally about the general decline in ethical behavior of the policy makers in the United States, but also has made it abundantly clear that after the 2007–2009 recession, major American economic journals have once again failed to alert public policy makers about the real cost consequences of such unethical behavior that have the potential to spill over national boundaries. As state tax amnesties were unravelling during 2009–2011, what became obvious to me was that as some policy makers showed blindfold confidence in the extant literature, it would only lead to a policy failure. State tax amnesties have proved that if the information received by governments for policy formulation was incorrect or of dubious quality, the policy decisions made by governments would be equally poor. I therefore decided to write this book to inform general public about my research.

In the combined form, the book offers a simple message that state tax amnesties are just another example of policy failure. The study of tax amnesty is of great importance in economics in that the orthodox approach of analyzing tax amnesties led to misleading policy implications that need to be replaced. Writing this book is also important because in the peer review process for the journal articles, I have gained several interesting insights into the cointegration analysis—the dominant paradigm in empirical time series economic research, which I plan to pursue in future research.

Finally, I received several emails from around the world showing interest in my research on tax amnesty. This provided me with additional motivation to continue in my efforts to get this book published. In fact, I would be truly happy if ordinary people in the United States and around world believe that this book indeed contributes not only to tax amnesty but also to the economics literature in general.

Hari Luitel, Ph.D.

Acknowledgment

The research for this book started as an independent study in the Fall Semester of 2002 when I was a graduate student at West Virginia University. Due to the scope of study, the research idea was subsequently developed into Ph.D. Thesis. Over the years, several chapters of the book were presented at many conferences. Below is the list in chronological order:

- "Revenue Impact of Repeated Tax Amnesties." Association for Budgeting and Financial Management, 16th Annual Conference, October 7–9, 2004, Chicago, Illinois.
- "Tax Amnesties and Compliance in the Long Run: A Time Series Analysis Revisited." Association for Budgeting and Financial Management, 17th Annual Conference, November 9–13, 2005, Washington DC.
- "Tax Amnesties and Compliance in the Long Run: A Time Series Analysis Revisited." National Tax Association, 98th Annual Conference, November 17–19, 2005, Miami, Florida.
- "Short-run and Long-run Effects of Tax Amnesties on Tax Revenues: Evidences from US States." National Tax Association, 100th Annual Conference, November 15–17, 2007, Columbus, Ohio.

- "Causes of State Tax Amnesties: Evidence from US States." National Tax Association, 101st Annual Conference, November 20–22, 2008, Philadelphia, PA.
- "An Examination of the Relation between State Fiscal Health and Amnesty Enactment." Western Economic Association International, 85th Annual conference, June 29 to July 2, 2010, Portland, Oregon.
- "A Reexamination of State Fiscal Health and Amnesty Enactment." Canadian Economic Association, 46th Annual Conference, June 7–10, 2012, Calgary.
- "Is a Tax Amnesty a Good Fiscal Policy? A Review of State Experience in the USA." Canadian Economic Association, 47th Annual Conference, May 30–June 2, 2013, Montreal.
- "Sensitivity of Assumption in Duration Analysis." Canadian Economic Association, 47th Annual Conference, May 30–June 2, 2013, Montreal.
- "Sensitivity of Assumption in Duration Analysis." Canadian Econometric Study Group, 30th Annual Meeting, October 18–20, 2013, Kitchener.

I thank discussants and all participants in the above conferences for their helpful comments and suggestions.

The book combines five articles—three of them were jointly coauthored. First article was written with Russell S. Sobel, second article with Mehmet S. Tosun and third one with Gerry J. Mahar. I am deeply indebted to all of my coauthors, without their support at various stages of writing this book would not have been possible.

I thank John Wiley & Sons, Inc., the National Tax Association and Springer for their liberal copyright policy and allowing me to adapt part of the articles entitled, "The Revenue Impact of Repeated Tax Amnesties," published in *Public Budgeting and Finance* Fall 2007, Vol. 27, Issue 3, pages 19-38, "Short-run and Long-run Effects of Tax Amnesties on Tax Revenues: Evidences from US States," published in *Proceedings of the Hundredth Annual Conference on*

Taxation (Washington, DC: National Tax Association, 2007), pages 402–413 and "A Reexamination of State Fiscal Health and Amnesty Enactment" forthcoming in *International Tax and Public Finance*.

Finally, I thank Brandon Mackinnon, a fourth year BBA student in economics at Algoma University, for his outstanding research assistance in the final revision of the book. I also express my sincere thanks to Joseph Perry, Laura Reiter and Scott Lutsky for their behind the scene help in the editorial process at Rowman & Littlefield Publishing Group. Their input has strengthened the book in many ways and I appreciate it. I am solely responsible for the remaining error.

Hari S. Luitel, Ph.D.
Sault Ste. Marie, 2014

1

Introduction

A relatively recent development in state government finances, tax amnesties are an interesting and intriguing phenomenon. Although governments of all types around the world have used tax amnesties as part of their fiscal program, the tax amnesty experience of state governments in the United States has been rather unique in terms of the frequency and variation in characteristics. Most but not all state governments rely on income taxes as a major source of their general fund revenues. Ensuring that citizens pay their taxes requires states to spend funds to deter noncompliance, detect its magnitude, and prosecute tax evaders. Yet, from an economic point of view, these government expenditures are inefficient in that they represent a real resource cost, while any additional revenues generated are simply a transfer of resources from the private to the public sector (Alm 2005). Rather than spending additional resources on tax enforcement, states may at times decide to offer tax amnesties to their citizens. Tax amnesties are government programs that usually grant immunity from legal prosecution and offer reduced financial penalties to tax evaders who voluntarily pay outstanding tax liabilities and interest, typically within a short period of time.

At one time, tax amnesties were considered to be a tool used for chronically non-compliant taxpayers in European and/or in developing countries. US tax authorities were principally concerned with the negative consequences of voluntary compliance, especially if tax payers developed an expectation that the next amnesty might be just on the horizon (Mikesell and Ross 2012). Beset by declining tax revenues and by mounting public expenditures, many state governments used tax amnesties as an alternative and a novel source of tax revenue (Alm, McKee, and Beck 1990). Especially, the recessions of 2001 and 2007–2009, led to an increase in the frequency of use of state tax amnesties due, in part, to general public opposition to statutory increases in tax rates. According to Federation of Tax Administrators (FTA), between 2001 and 2012 alone, the combined fifty states offered a total of sixty-five amnesties—an average of 5.4 tax amnesties per year.[1] In a recent review of the structural evolution of US state amnesties, Mikesell and Ross (2012) argue that tax amnesties have become a tool for tax revenue collection that many states often pursue even at the expense of the existing systems of tax administration. Is a tax amnesty a good tax policy? To address this question, this book reexamines the proposition whether a typical state tax amnesty is likely to generate substantial short-term tax revenues without a corresponding significant negative effect on long-run tax compliance.

Although US states have several motivations for implementing tax amnesties (Ross 1986, Parle and Hirlinger 1986), the underlying objective boils down to raising tax revenues, either through the taxes collected immediately or through additions of new tax payers to the tax rolls and through an enlarged tax base. Are state tax amnesties successful in achieving this basic objective (i.e., bringing revenues to the state treasury that would not otherwise be collected)? This book revisits this critical question, given the significant fiscal crisis that many state governments have confronted since the turn of the twenty-first century.[2]

The plan of the book is as follows: chapter 2 describes the tax amnesty controversy, and provides the rationale for the need of present study. Chapter 3 reviews the relevant literature. Chapter 4 discusses the tax amnesty experience of selected countries worldwide. Chapter 5 reviews the experience of state tax amnesty in the United States, while chapter 6 reviews the specific experience of Colorado's 1985 tax amnesty. Chapter 7 reviews the causes of state tax amnesties. Chapter 8 presents empirical analysis and results. Discussion and conclusion follow in chapter 9.

NOTES

1. These numbers exclude tax amnesties enacted by City of New York, District of Columbia, and other local or territorial jurisdictions.

2. The fundamental problem that leads to state government fiscal crisis is cyclical variability in the revenue stream. As long as revenue shows stable growth from year to year, fiscal crises do not appear, but slowdowns in revenue growth produce a widespread crisis atmosphere (Holcombe and Sobel 1997).

2

Tax Amnesty Controversy and Rationale for the Need of Present Study

In recent years, state governments in the United States have frequently used tax amnesties to generate tax revenues (Mikesell and Ross 2012). For our review purpose, tax amnesties refer to state tax policies employed to collect overdue taxes.[1] According to National Association of State Budget Officers [NASBO] (2004), participants in tax amnesty programs agree to pay, within a short time period, past-due taxes and fees but escape paying fines or interest on taxes owed. In return, the state promises not to file criminal or civil charges against these individuals or corporations.

The practice of offering tax amnesties has generated substantial controversy. For the early debate, see Jackson (1986); Lerman (1986); Leonard and Zeckhauser (1986); Dubin, Graetz, and Wilde (1992); and Alm and Beck (1993). For the recent debate, see Luitel (2007), Luitel and Sobel (2007); Luitel (2013); and Luitel and Tosun (2013). Proponents argue that tax amnesties are a "costless tax." States collect tax revenues without incurring enforcement costs because individual participation in an amnesty is voluntary. Some tax evaders may wish to rejoin or to comply more fully with the tax law but do not due to punitive fines and public embarrassment that would likely result if their tax evasion were found out. If a tax amnesty were offered, these people could rejoin the tax collection system without fines and public embarrassment. Tax amnesties thus represent arguably a *Pareto improvement* because these people gain, no one else loses, and state tax authorities collect more tax revenues in the short term from overdue taxes and by bringing delinquent tax payers back into the tax system over the long term.

Opponents question whether a tax amnesty really does produce any additional tax revenue. They argue that tax officials are simply collecting tax revenues that would have been collected by normal enforcement procedures. Opponents also contend that tax amnesties provide incentives for compliant taxpayers to begin to evade taxes in anticipation of a future tax amnesty. This situation may weaken tax compliance and foster a public perception of inefficiency in tax collection and enforcement in the tax system. See table 2.1 for a more detailed listing of the most common arguments for and against tax amnesties.

Many of the early investigations of tax amnesties noted that state tax authorities offered tax amnesties as a means of improving operations of the tax administration system (Mikesell 1986, Ross 1986, Parle and Hirlinger 1986). A recent review of the structural evolution of all state amnesty programs showed that the initial purpose of state tax amnesties has shifted away from improving the internal tax administration process to an emphasis on maximization of tax revenue collections (Mikesell and Ross 2012). This change in purpose serves as one motivation to update our knowledge about what is known in the tax amnesty literature. A review of US state amnesty experience is appropriate for a number of reasons: firstly, many observers consider the purpose of contemporary tax amnesties to be different today than thirty years ago. Secondly, it is plausible that in a crisis-like atmosphere due to a slowdown in tax revenue collections that US state tax authorities experienced in the 1980s or 2000s could occur again and again in the future. Thirdly, as I review international tax amnesty experiences in chapter 4, it is also quite plausible that countries around the world could experience similar conditions that caused states to offer tax amnesties. Last but not least, in an integrated global economy, when real costs of a policy

Table 2.1. Arguments in Favor and Against Tax Amnesties

	Arguments in Favor:		Arguments Against:
1.	Pareto improving because nobody looses and government increases revenue.	1.	Undermines tax morale, as honest taxpayers may get upset because moral costs to behave dishonestly decrease.
2.	Brings people back to the path of honesty who became tax delinquents or evaders by mistake.	2.	Too soft an action to be taken against law breakers.
3.	Removes the guilty feeling of otherwise ordinary citizens.	3.	Guilty feeling is removed such that honest taxpayers may actually start evading taxes.
4.	Most appropriate before increasing penalties and enforcement and to the transition to a new tax regime.	4.	Individuals become aware of the presence of rampant non-compliance in the tax system.
5.	Signals that the government is committed to tackle the problem of tax evasion.	5.	Sends a wrong signal of a weak enforcement that the government is unable to enforce the tax code.
6.	Enlarges the tax base as many taxpayers are brought back into the tax system.	6.	Taxpayers would anticipate future tax amnesties, which will have a negative effect on timely tax compliance and erodes the tax base.
7.	Generates both short run and long run revenues for the government.	7.	Experience indicates that amnesties produce little and/or overstated revenues.
8.	Reduces administrative costs of tax collection.	8.	Tax revenues could have been collected with the normal enforcement procedure anyway if waited a little longer
9.	Enhances tax compliance by keeping and monitoring taxpayers not previously on the tax rolls.	9.	Simply not possible. If it were true, then the amnesty is not required in the first place.

failure have the potential to spill over national boundaries, a critical examination of what goes on in any country (and particularly in the United States) is timely.

NOTE

1. For various types of tax amnesty, see Joint Committee on Taxation [JCS-2-98] (1998).

3

Literature Review

Within the standard expected-utility model of tax evasion, it is a puzzle why a tax evader would participate in a tax amnesty. The model clearly predicts that amnesties would have no effect on the behavior of delinquent taxpayers. If an individual evaluates the costs and benefits of evasion, and makes the decision to evade taxes, this decision would be unaffected by the announcement of the amnesty because it doesn't change the expected marginal costs and expected marginal benefits of evasion. This puzzle has been addressed by Malik and Schwab (1991) who show that in an adaptive utility framework, where a taxpayer learns about his or her utility function through experience, the decision to evade could be affected by offering a tax amnesty now that their utility function has been internally updated with revised calculated risks. Furthermore, in practice, amnesties are generally offered in conjunction with an announcement of increased enforcement. The threat of higher enforcement effort in the near future (and the higher expected cost of evasion it entails) works as an additional incentive for an evader to participate in an amnesty program.

Alm and Beck (1990, 1991) and Andreoni (1991) have theoretically analyzed the impact of tax amnesties from a different perspective. Alm and Beck (1990, 1991) show that amnesties may sometimes increase compliance and tax collections, especially if individuals perceive paying taxes is the social norm and the amnesty is accompanied by heightened enforcement efforts. However, short-run amnesty revenues may come at the expense of reduced long-run tax revenues because of the permanent reduction in tax compliance. The authors conclude that although tax amnesties generate short-term revenues, their ability to generate revenues in the long run is ambiguous. Andreoni (1991), on the other hand, examines fully anticipated tax amnesties and finds that evasion rises as a result of the amnesty but tax revenue does not necessarily fall. This is because evasion rises only to the extent that people expect to participate in the amnesty and if they participate in the amnesty, then the government is able to recapture not only the new evasion but also the pre-existing evasion. If the initial evasion is large, then the amnesty may increase tax revenue even if there is an increase in evasion.

Usually, the measure of success (or desirability) of a tax amnesty was tax revenue yield, the number of participants and their retention in the tax system. Using experimental methods, Alm, McKee, and Beck (1990) examined the long-run effects of a tax amnesty, and found that tax compliance fell after an amnesty unless post-amnesty enforcement efforts were increased. The Joint Committee on Taxation [JCS-2-98] (1998) interpreted the second amnesty in Connecticut to have been consistent with these results. Studies on cross-country experiments in Switzerland and in Costa Rica showed that long-run tax compliance would rise if the proposed tax amnesty were voted on, regardless of whether the amnesty was passed or rejected. These studies also showed that anticipation of a future tax amnesty had a negative effect on tax compliance (Torgler and Schaltegger, 2005 and Torgler, Schaltegger, and Schaffner, 2003). For policy purposes, however, experimental studies provide an incomplete guide to the likely effect of a tax amnesty on tax revenues.

On the empirical front, opinions vary widely over the usefulness of amnesties to collect tax revenues both in the short-term and long-term. Of the few empirical studies that actually examined the taxes collected during and after the amnesty period question the ability of a tax amnesty to collect additional tax revenues. The analysis of the

1986 Michigan amnesty revealed that most non-filers were out of compliance for a single year before the amnesty. A small number of taxpayers in Michigan evaded a large amount of taxes over longer time periods and most taxpayers in Michigan used the tax amnesty to repay relatively small amounts of overdue taxes (Fisher, Goddeeris, and Young 1989). Similarly, the analysis of the data for the 1983 Massachusetts tax amnesty showed that chronic evaders and evaders who paid taxes but underreported generally did not participate in the amnesty program (Joulfaian 1988). These findings were at odds with the claim that amnesties would bring chronic tax evaders back into the tax system. In a separate study of the 1986 Michigan amnesty, Christian, Gupta, and Young (2002) found that while a substantial portion of participants in the amnesty continued to pay taxes after the amnesty, the amnesty's impact on tax revenue was negligible. These findings contradict those that claim tax amnesties do generate substantial tax revenues for state treasury.

Two pioneering works that played an important role in the public policy debate over state tax amnesties were Dubin, Graetz, and Wilde (1992) and Alm and Beck (1993).[1] Based on the assumption of normally distributed hazards, Dubin, Graetz and Wilde (1992) analyzed the initial wave of state tax amnesties, and concluded that states were likely to enact tax amnesties when they were most likely to be effective in generating additional tax revenues. Analyzing the 1985 Colorado tax amnesty, Alm and Beck (1993) concluded that the amnesty had no long-run impact on the level or the trend of tax collections. These studies together imply that tax amnesties tend to generate a higher tax revenue yield without any overall negative consequences on future tax payer compliance. The apparently misleading implication of these studies cannot be ruled out not to have influenced the tax policies of US states in recent years. Thus, to get to the bottom of these misleading sources and fix them, I will spend some time to critically evaluate both of these studies and to highlight a new and alternative interpretation of the research results. To do so, chapter 6 will provide a critique on Alm and Beck's 1993 paper and chapter 7 will provide a critique on Dubin, Graetz, and Wilde's 1992 paper. These chapters contribute to the literature on tax amnesty by pointing out to an apparently misleading tax policy implication that would otherwise remain unreported.

NOTE

1. The papers by Dubin, Graetz, and Wilde (1992) and by Alm and Beck (1993) appeared in *Quarterly Journal of Economics* and *National Tax Journal*, both of which consistently rank high among the economic journals (Liebowitz and Palmer 1984; Kalaitzidakis, Mamuneas, and Stengos 2011). Thus, any claim that these papers absolutely did not have any effect in the public policy discourse would be tantamount to "failure to see through indirectedness." (For several examples of failure to see through indirectedness, see Gino, Moore, and Bazerman 2008.) Moreover, most scholars would like to see the influence of one's ideas: having other scholars base their work on those ideas, having students learn from them, and having public policy influenced by them. This is particularly true in economics discipline (Hammermesh 2007). From these points of view, both of these papers are highly influential.

4

A Review of International Tax Amnesty Experience

Following the suit of the state governments in the United States, many developed countries and developing countries have conducted tax amnesties as part of their fiscal program. For example, Argentina, France, India, Ireland, and Italy have offered tax amnesties for a number of times and sometimes the repetition of amnesty took place at an interval as short as every two years. Just like the US states, some of these countries have made repeated use of amnesties. The terms and conditions of tax amnesties vary from country to country. Many countries have had tax amnesties, both general amnesties and specifically targeted tax amnesties. Some amnesties have not only abated penalties but also interest and even liabilities for tax. For example, the Venezuela tax amnesty (1996) reduced tax liabilities of participating taxpayers by 75 percent and, the Panama tax amnesty (1974) reduced tax liabilities by 80 percent for tax payers. Many amnesties have allowed taxpayers with accounts receivable or in civil tax litigation to participate in the programs. For example, the Argentina tax amnesty (1995) allowed taxpayers involved in criminal tax proceedings to participate in the amnesty. Likewise, amnesty collection amount across countries varies widely. For example, the general amnesty in Argentina (1995) yielded about $3.9 billion in tax collected, the general amnesty in India (1993) yielded about $2.5 billion in tax collected and the Irish amnesty (1988) yielded more than $700 million in tax collected.[1] Tax amnesty experience of selected countries is discussed briefly below.

Argentina:

With an objective to encourage repatriation of capital flight, Argentina ran a tax amnesty in 1987 for its citizens and for foreign nationals. As part of its debt-to-equity program, the amnesty exempted from taxes all previously unreported income used for business investment purposes. Moreover, the tax amnesty also promised not to investigate the origin of funds or to prosecute delinquent Argentine taxpayers. The only condition set for the amnesty was that for every dollar of debt converted into equity, the investor would be required to make a matching contribution of an additional dollar in new investment funds, and the new investment funds so raised were to be used to purchase new equipment, to build new plants, or to improve the physical capacity of existing plant and facilities. Argentina had a history of several tax amnesties, and the 1987 amnesty was not accompanied by any stricter enforcement efforts or changes in the tax code. Consequently, it brought no additional revenues to the government and was widely viewed as policy failure (Uchitelle 1989, Alm 1998).

Belgium:

With an objective to attract flight capital and black market funds to bring back into the regular economy, Belgium offered a tax amnesty in 1984. The tax amnesty exempted capital from taxes if the capital was invested in employment-generating activities before the end of 1984. The amnesty also waived any obligation to report the origin or source of the funds provided that one-eleventh, or 9 percent, of the amount in question was invested in five-year non-interest-bearing treasury certificates. However, the government in 1985 faced a number of political problems, and was compelled to rescind the amnesty legislation (Uchitelle 1989).

Colombia:

Colombia ran a tax amnesty in 1987. The tax amnesty allowed taxpayers who had previously failed to report or who over reported their liabilities to correct their tax reports without being subject to further investigation. Known tax delinquents were excluded from participating in the tax amnesty. To be eligible for the amnesty, taxpayers had to declare their income at least as high as their reported income in the previous years. The tax amnesty was also accompanied by many changes in the tax system. For example, the government reduced the income tax rates, increased income tax withholding rates and eliminated the double taxation of dividends. Administrative practices such as enforcement of the tax code and penalties detected for post amnesty tax evasion were also increased. The amnesty collected about $94 million, or about 0.3 percent of GDP in 1987 (Uchitelle 1989, Alm 1998).

Costa Rica:

In considering tax reform that included a tax amnesty, the Congress of Costa Rica approved a tax contingency law in December 2000. The President sanctioned the bill on December 18 and it became effective on January 1, 2003. The reform consisted, among others, increases in the income tax rate, the corporate tax rate, the property tax rate. The tax amnesty allowed tax payers a two month time period to clear up tax liabilities for taxes managed by the tax authorities. These included income tax, sales tax, selective consumption tax, property tax on vehicles, transfer tax of real property and vehicles, education and culture stamp tax, tax on offshore companies, taxes on gambling houses, specific tax on alcoholic beverage etc. Costa Rica had previously offered a tax amnesty in 1995 (Torgler, Schaltegger, and Schaffner 2003).

France:

France also has made repeated use of tax amnesty as part of its fiscal policy.[2] With an objective to stimulate repatriation of illegally held capital abroad, France ran in 1982 a general tax amnesty as well as a specific tax amnesty program. The general tax amnesty applied to all income and value-added taxes. About 2,786 people participated in the general amnesty and paid $19 million. Similarly, about 276 people participated in the special program to repatriate capital and this amnesty brought back about $22 million. However, these programs were not considered as successful partly due to the high wealth tax prevailing in France in 1982.

In 1986, France offered a tax amnesty for a second time. Like the previous tax amnesty, the objective of this amnesty was to recoup income illegally transferred abroad. The tax rate was significantly reduced from 25 percent in 1982 to 10 percent in 1986 on repatriated capital as well as the wealth tax was also abolished. These additional measures were taken to address the sources of the failure of 1982 amnesty. Enforcement, however, was not increased after the amnesty and the amount of exact tax amnesty collection was not known but was believed to be small.

India:

India is one of the countries that has frequently used tax amnesties as a fiscal policy tool. Of the many amnesties offered, two important and often cited ones were conducted in 1981 and 1997 will be briefly discussed here.[3]

In February 1981, India ran a tax amnesty for about three months. The amnesty was considered unique because the government issued special bearer bonds with the objective to tap into untaxed income. Targeted people, holding undisclosed incomes, were allowed to purchase these bonds and were promised by the government not to investigate the origin of the funds. The money invested in special bearer bonds was exempted from all types of taxes. The tax amnesty enabled the government to collect over one billion dollars from these bonds. After the conclusion of the amnesty, the tax structure did not change and tax enforcement was not increased. The amnesty therefore was not considered successful because it did not raise as much tax revenue as anticipated nor did it enlarge the overall tax base of India.

From July to December 1997, India ran another tax amnesty for 214 days with a slogan *"30 percent taxes, 100 percent peace of mind."* The amnesty offered a large element of forgiveness to tax evaders. Unlike previous tax amnesties, this tax amnesty was extensively publicized in different forms of media, for example, radio, television, and newspaper, with an emphasis that the amnesty would be the last of its kind and enforcement would be increased at the end of the tax amnesty. About 350,000 people participated in the tax amnesty and $2.5 billion was collected of which approximately one half was from individual income tax. This was considered to be one of the most successful tax amnesties.

Ireland:

Ireland has made repeated use of tax amnesties—five amnesties in six years between two general amnesties in 1988 and 1993.[4] The first general tax amnesty of Ireland was run from January to October 1988. It allowed taxpayers a period of ten months to pay taxes without incurring any interests, tax penalties, civil or criminal lawsuits. The amnesty was publicized as one time opportunity only and at the end of the amnesty, enforcement of the tax code was increased. Moreover, the overall tax structure was reformed. Tax authorities expected to raise $50 million dollars and the tax revenue collection actually exceeded over $700 million dollars. The amnesty was considered successful for the following reasons: (i) It was the first amnesty in Ireland. (ii) The amnesty was well publicized as the last opportunity for delinquent tax payers to be forgiven. (iii) Post-amnesty enforcement of tax code was increased and the tax structure was reformed. (iv) Penalty for the detected post-amnesty tax evasion was increased. (v) During the amnesty the government actually started publishing in the national newspapers lists of the names of people who were delinquent in their tax payments.

Although the 1988 amnesty was publicized as the first and last opportunity, Ireland encountered with a serious budget deficit when it announced, in 1993, a special amnesty with the objective to stimulate repatriation of undeclared income from abroad. The special amnesty waived all penalties and interest and promised confidentiality of the source of the fund. The repatriated funds were subject to a special low rate of 15 percent, in contrast to normal rate, which was above 50 percent. However, the parliamentary opposition parties and trade unions criticized the amnesty as a concession to the wealthy few taxpayers. The government, then, responded by adopting a general amnesty which offered abatement of both penalties and interest but liabilities were not reduced. The 1993 amnesty was considered unsuccessful because the revenue collected was reported to be significantly lower than the revenue collected for the 1988 general amnesty.

Italy:

Italy has most frequently used tax amnesties in the contemporary period. It offered four general amnesties and numerous specific tax amnesties usually by decree since 1973. Four general amnesties were held in 1973, 1982, 1991, and 2003. They were all similar in nature and characteristics. These amnesties provided full tax relief of previously undeclared taxes. Taxpayers without any new declarations of tax base but only by paying a fixed percentage of the gross tax already paid could benefit the total exemptions from future inspection. Tax collections in Italian amnesties had not been encouraging. For the general amnesty in 1982, the Italian government expected to raise $4.6 billion in tax revenues but actual tax collections were far less than anticipated at approximately $700,000. Tax amnesties had occurred so regularly in Italy that the expectation of future amnesties had been cited as a factor in the low national level of tax compliance (JCS-2-98 1998, Marè and Salleo 2003).

New Zealand:

New Zealand ran a tax amnesty in 1988. Unlike amnesties in other countries where penalties for tax offences are generally increased only after the amnesty period is over, New Zealand considerably strengthened penalties for tax offences two years prior to the amnesty. Late payment penalty was still charged even if tax amnesty was granted to the taxpayers. Late filing penalty was considered as a charge against the use of the time value of money, otherwise amnesty participants would have been effectively paying lower taxes than taxpayers who paid their taxes on time. The amnesty promised that taxpayers would not be subject to investigation just because they participated in the amnesty. Nonetheless, a full disclosure from each taxpayer participating in the amnesty was required. About 16,000 participants filed 24,685 amnesty returns that resulted in total tax assessed of USD 26.6 million and USD 3 million in refund, with most returns relating to income tax (Hasseldine 1998).

Russia:

During the entire transition period, Russia experienced tax problems such as lagging in tax collections as well as wide spread tax evasion.[5] Therefore, with an objective of reforming the tax system, Russia has enacted tax amnesties a number of times since 1992. Russia ran its first amnesty from October 27 to November 30, 1993. The amnesty waived any penalties on the unpaid liabilities if participating enterprises, organizations and private entrepreneurs disclosed their unpaid taxes and tax payments for 1993 and all preceding years. After the amnesty, the penalty for the detected tax evasion was increased by three times of the unpaid tax liability. However, the amnesty was not successful because the design of the amnesty was considered flawed and it was criticized for having the timeframe of one month to repay tax liabilities too short and not allowing for inadvertent or unintended mistakes. As such, the 1993 amnesty was repealed in 1995.

Russia ran a second amnesty again on January 16, 1996, that was later amended on April 22, 1996. The second amnesty allowed enterprises and organizations with tax arrears to defer their payments provided that they timely paid all current payments in full. Enterprises and organizations that were granted deferments were required to pay 50 percent of the total amount due by October 1998, with the quarterly payments of 5 percent of the liabilities. A 30 percent annual interest rate was charged on the unpaid amounts. The remaining 50 percent deferment liability could be paid over the following five years in equal payments without any interest charge. However, the requirement of 50 percent of the arrears to be paid by October 1998, with the remaining 50 percent subject to an annual interest rate of 30 percent was impractical. Nonetheless, the amnesty was continued in somewhat modified form by additional presidential decrees, which also contained provisions such as reduced interest penalties on late payments and on tax arrears and an allowance for unintended mistakes in the preparation of tax returns, all of which were intended to reduce the burden of tax payment. Moreover, also the tax authorities were expected to increase the frequency of tax audits.

In summary, the Russian tax amnesties were not successful. Given the poor quality of tax administration in Russia, these amnesties and related provisions were seen by tax officials as easy ways of dealing with delinquent tax liabilities, especially those of mounting tax arrears. Furthermore, the almost yearly enactment of some form of amnesty contributed to the widespread belief that they would be a regular event.

Switzerland:

After the Second World War, Switzerland ran three general tax amnesties at the national level.[6] In 1940, trying to find new ways to finance the defense costs that incurred during the World War II, the Swiss government levied an extraordinary property tax as a one-time charge. Although new federal taxes needed to pass by a popular referendum, the cabinet used its extended legal power at war time and enacted the new tax by decree. The revenue collection from such type of amnesty was not successful.

Switzerland ran its second general amnesty in 1944. It was accompanied by stricter enforcement of the tax code and an exchange of information between national and sub-national tax authorities. This amnesty was considered to be successful.

In the early 1960s, tax amnesty at the federal level surfaced again. Although the federal government didn't like the idea of the amnesty without increasing the enforcement, the parliament proposed a bill for tax amnesty, which was defeated in the 1964 popular referendum. Subsequently, the proposal was modified and re-forwarded for referendum which was then approved by a majority of the votes.

Very recently, countries like Great Britain conducted a series of tax amnesties to the administration of the VAT, and Germany used tax amnesty in advance of pursuing tax evaders appearing on a list of "tax haven accounts" from Swiss banks. Given their prevalence in countries from every continent, analysis of tax amnesty is important because our knowledge on the compliance effect of an amnesty in terms of revenue potential is far from conclusive (Mikesell and Ross 2012).

NOTES

1. See United States Congress, JCS-2-98 (1998) and Alm (1998).

2. See also Alm (1998), Hasseldine (1998), JCS-2-98 (1998), and Uchitelle (1989).

3. See also Alm (1998), Torgler and Schaltegger (2005), and Uchitelle (1989).

4. See also Alm (1998), Hasseldine (1998), JCS-2-98 (1998), and Uchitelle (1989).

5. See Alm, Martinez-Vazques, and Wallace (2000).

6. See Torgler and Schaltegger (2005), and Torgler, Schaltegger, and Schaffner (2003).

5

A Review of US State
Tax Amnesty Experience

Although the US federal government held a permanent tax amnesty program between 1919 and 1952, and since 1961 there has been some form of informal voluntary disclosure program, state tax amnesties have rebounded in popularity after the turn of the twenty-first century.[1] Based on data compiled by the Federation of Tax Administrators (FTA), Arizona appears to be the first state to have enacted a tax amnesty in 1982. Since then, forty-five states and the District of Columbia have enacted tax amnesties: these have occurred in several waves, in the early to mid-1980s, the late-1990s, and during and after the 2001 and 2008 recessions. Some states have offered tax amnesties more than once. Table 5.1 presents the frequency with which states offered tax amnesties between 1982 and 2011, and figure 5.1 illustrates the number of amnesties offered each year. Notice that the frequency of tax amnesties rose during and after the 2001 and 2008 recessions. In fact, in 2009 alone, states offered twelve amnesties, with nine of these reflecting amnesties that were repeated for a second, third, fourth, or even fifth time. These broad-based amnesties typically included all major state taxes but some excluded property tax, motor fuel tax, or other taxes.

Table 5.2 summarizes the main features of state tax amnesties and shows that a majority of state amnesties (92 out of 111) were approved through legislative authorization and sixty-one out of 111

Table 5.1.   Tax Amnesties Offered by the States (as of December 2011)

Number of Amnesties Offered	Number of States	States
None	5	Alaska[a,c], Montana[c], Tennessee[a], Utah, Wyoming[a,b]
One	11	Delaware[c] (2009), Georgia (1992), Hawaii (2009), Idaho (1983), Indiana (2005), Minnesota (1984), Nebraska (2004), North Carolina (1989), Oregon[c] (2009), South Dakota[a,b] (1999), Washington[a,b] (2011)
Two	14	Alabama (1984, 2009), Arkansas (1987, 2004), California (1984/85, 2005), Iowa (1986, 2007), Kentucky (1988, 2002), Mississippi (1986, 2004), New Hampshire[a,c] (1997/98, 2001/02), North Dakota (1983, 2003/04), Ohio (2001/02, 2006), Pennsylvania (1995/96, 2010), South Carolina (1985, 2002), Vermont (1990, 2009), West Virginia (1986, 2004), Wisconsin (1985, 1998)
Three	13	Colorado (1985, 2003, 2011), Illinois (1984, 2003, 2010), Kansas (1984, 2003, 2010), Maine (1990, 2003, 2009), Maryland (1987, 2001, 2009), Michigan (1986, 2002, 2011), Missouri (1983, 2002, 2003), Nevada[a,b] (2002, 2008, 2010), New Mexico (1985, 1999, 2010), Oklahoma (1984, 2002, 2008), Rhode Island (1986/87, 1996, 2006), Texas[a,b] (1984, 2004, 2007), Virginia (1990, 2003, 2009)
Four	5	Arizona (1982/83, 2002, 2003, 2009), Connecticut[d] (1990, 1995, 2002, 2009), Florida[a] (1987, 1988, 2003, 2010), Massachusetts (1983/84, 2002, 2003, 2010), New Jersey (1987, 1996, 2002, 2009)
Five	2	Louisiana (1985, 1987, 1998, 2001, 2009), New York (1985/86, 1996/97, 2002/03, 2005/06, 2010)

Notes:
a: no personal income tax
b: no corporate income tax
c: no general sales tax
d: Connecticut introduced a personal income tax in 1991.

Source: FTA, *http://www.taxadmin.org/fta/rate/amnesty1.html*. Web access date: 07/26/2012.

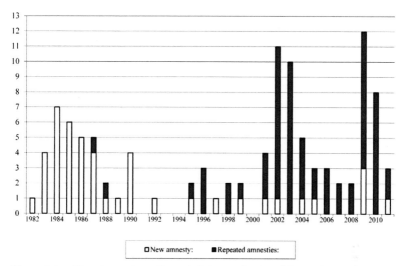

Figure 5.1.   New Amnesty vs. Repeated Amnesties (as of December 2011).
FTA, http://www.taxadmin.org/fta/rate/amnesty1.html. Web access date: 07/26/2012.

amnesties allowed delinquent tax payers identified by the tax authorities to participate in the program. Thirty-five out of 111 amnesties permitted taxes to be paid in installments and fifty out of 111 amnesties did not provide any arrangements.

Table 5.3 provides listing of the state tax amnesties between 1982 and 2012. The period of tax amnesty varied widely among states. For the period 1982–2012, Kentucky conducted the shortest amnesty lasting only fifteen days in 1988 while Oklahoma, in 1983, and Arkansas, in 1984, offered the longest amnesty at 183 days. Data on tax amnesty collection in current dollars reveals a large variation in short-term revenue yield among states. Twenty-four out of 111 state tax amnesties were reported to collecte short-run revenues equal to or greater than $100 million and ten states generated $1 million or less. Though not unimportant, these tax amnesty collections were small relative to total state tax collections. For example, the table also shows that between 1982 and 2012, tax amnesties collected

Table 5.2. Characteristics of State Tax Amnesties (1982–2012)

	Number of Amnesties with Legislative Authorization	Number of Amnesties that Included Accounts Receivable[§]	Number of Amnesties that Permitted Installment Arrangements
Yes	92	61	35
No	10	33	50
No information[§§]	9	18	26

Source: FTA, September 2012. *http://www.taxadmin.org/fta/rate/amnesty1.pdf.*
Web access date: February 17, 2013.

Notes: [§] The 1984-85 California amnesty allowed known delinquents of individual income taxes to participate in the amnesty but it didn't allow known delinquents of sales taxes to participate in the amnesty. Therefore, it is counted twice in this category.
[§§] Information on amnesty characteristics was not available from the FTA.

average taxes below 1 percent (only 0.74 percent) and not more than 3 percent of total state tax revenue. These short-run revenue gains often come at the expense of long-run revenue losses due to reduced future compliance by taxpayers attributable to the amnesty. Unfortunately, this fact so far has been ignored by the architect of state tax amnesties.

Table 5.3. State Tax Amnesty Periods and Ranking of Amnesty Collections (1982–2012)

Name of State	Amnesty Period Begin	End	Days	Amnesty Collection in current $ (Millions)	Rank	Percent of State Total Tax Revenue	Rank
(1)	(2)	(3)	(4)	(5)	(6)	(7)	(8)
ALABAMA							
First amnesty	1/20/1984	4/1/1984	72	3.2	78	0.12%	73
Second amnesty	2/1/2009	5/15/2009	103	8.1	68	0.10%	74
ARIZONA							
First amnesty	11/22/1982	1/20/1983	59	6.0	77	0.29%	54
Second amnesty	1/1/2002	2/28/2002	58	N/A			
Third amnesty	9/1/2003	10/31/2003	60	73.0	31	0.84%	32
Fourth amnesty	5/1/2009	6/1/2009	31	32.0	49	0.29%	55
ARKANSAS							
First amnesty	9/1/1987	11/30/1987	90	1.7	80	0.09%	75
Second amnesty	7/1/2004	12/31/2004	183	N/A			
CALIFORNIA							
First amnesty	12/10/1984	3/15/1985	95	197.0	14	0.68%	37
Second amnesty	2/1/2005	3/31/2005	58	N/A			
COLORADO							
First amnesty	9/16/1985	11/15/1985	60	6.4	76	0.28%	56
Second amnesty	6/1/2003	6/30/2003	29	18.4	54	0.28%	58
Third amnesty	10/1/2011	11/15/2011	45	N/A			
CONNECTICUT							
First amnesty	9/1/1990	11/30/1990	90	54.0	35	1.03%	26
Second amnesty	9/1/1995	11/30/1995	90	46.2	39	0.62%	40
Third amnesty	9/1/2002	12/2/2002	92	109.0	19	1.21%	22
Fourth amnesty	5/1/2009	6/25/2009	55	40.0	41	0.33%	51
DELAWARE	9/1/2009	10/30/2009	59	N/A			
FLORIDA							
First amnesty	1/1/1987	6/30/1987	180	13.0	62	0.13%	72
Second amnesty	1/1/1988	6/30/1988	181	8.4	67	0.07%	78
Third amnesty	7/1/2003	10/31/2003	122	80.0	29	0.30%	53
Fourth amnesty	7/1/2010	9/30/2010	91	N/A			
GEORGIA	10/1/1992	12/5/1992	65	51.3	37	0.71%	36
HAWAII	5/27/2009	6/26/2009	30	14.0	57	0.30%	52
IDAHO	5/20/1983	8/30/1983	102	0.3	90	0.05%	84
ILLINOIS							
First amnesty	10/1/1984	11/30/1984	60	160.5	17	1.84%	10
Second amnesty	10/1/2003	11/17/2003	47	532.0	3	2.40%	6
Third amnesty	10/1/2010	11/8/2010	38	314.0	8	1.23%	21
INDIANA	9/15/2005	11/15/2005	61	255.0	12	1.98%	7
IOWA							
First amnesty	9/2/1986	10/31/1986	59	35.1	45	1.43%	15
Second amnesty	9/4/2007	10/31/2007	57	N/A			

(continued)

Table 5.3. *(Continued)*

Name of State (1)	Amnesty Period Begin (2)	End (3)	Days (4)	Amnesty Collection in current $ (Million) (5)	Rank (6)	Percent of State Total Tax Revenue (7)	Rank (8)
KANSAS							
First amnesty	7/1/1984	9/30/1984	91	0.6	87	0.03%	87
Second amnesty	10/1/2003	11/30/2003	60	53.7	36	1.07%	25
Third amnesty	9/1/2010	10/15/2010	44	N/A			
KENTUCKY							
First amnesty	9/15/1988	9/30/1988	15	100.0	21	2.73%	2
Second amnesty	8/1/2002	9/30/2002	60	100.0	22	1.25%	20
Third amnesty	10/1/2012	11/30/2012	60	N/A			
LOUISIANA							
First amnesty	10/1/1985	12/31/1985	91	1.2	82	0.03%	88
Second amnesty	10/1/1987	12/15/1987	75	0.3	91	0.01%	90
Third amnesty	10/1/1998	12/31/1998	91	1.3	81	0.02%	89
Fourth amnesty	9/1/2001	10/30/2001	59	192.9	15	2.68%	3
Fifth amnesty	9/1/2009	10/31/2009	60	303.7	9	2.98%	1
MAINE							
First amnesty	11/1/1990	12/31/1990	60	29.0	51	1.86%	9
Second amnesty	9/1/2003	11/30/2003	90	37.6	43	1.39%	16
Third amnesty	9/1/2009	11/30/2009	90	16.2	55	0.46%	49
MARYLAND							
First amnesty	9/1/1987	11/2/1987	62	34.6	46	0.66%	38
Second amnesty	9/1/2001	10/31/2001	60	39.2	42	0.36%	50
Third amnesty	9/1/2009	10/31/2009	60	9.6	66	0.06%	81
MASSACHUSETTS							
First amnesty	10/17/1983	1/17/1984	92	86.5	27	1.48%	14
Second amnesty	10/1/2002	11/30/2002	60	96.1	26	0.65%	39
Third amnesty	1/1/2003	2/28/2003	58	11.2	64	0.07%	79
Fourth amnesty	4/1/2010	6/1/2010	61	32.6	47	0.16%	69
MICHIGAN							
First amnesty	5/12/1986	6/30/1986	49	109.8	18	1.18%	23
Second amnesty	5/15/2002	6/30/2002	46	N/A			
Third amnesty	5/15/2011	6/30/2011	46	N/A			
MINNESOTA	8/1/1984	10/31/1984	91	12.1	63	0.24%	64
MISSISSIPPI							
First amnesty	9/1/1986	11/30/1986	90	1.0	83	0.05%	83
Second amnesty	9/1/2004	12/31/2004	121	7.9	69	0.15%	70
MISSOURI							
First amnesty	9/1/1983	10/31/1983	60	0.9	85	0.03%	86
Second amnesty	8/1/2002	10/31/2002	91	76.4	30	0.88%	29
Third amnesty	8/1/2003	10/31/2003	91	20.0	53	0.23%	66
NEBRASKA	8/1/2004	10/31/2004	91	7.5	71	0.21%	67
NEVADA							
First amnesty	2/1/2002	6/30/2002	149	7.3	72	0.19%	68
Second amnesty	7/1/2008	11/28/2008	150	N/A			
Third amnesty	7/1/2010	10/1/2010	92	N/A			

Name of State	Amnesty Period Begin	Amnesty Period End	Days	Amnesty Collection in current $ (Million)	Rank	Percent of State Total Tax Revenue	Rank
(1)	(2)	(3)	(4)	(5)	(6)	(7)	(8)
NEW HAMPSHIRE							
First amnesty	12/1/1997	2/17/1998	78	13.5	60	1.34%	18
Second amnesty	12/1/2001	2/15/2002	76	13.5	61	0.71%	35
NEW JERSEY							
First amnesty	9/10/1987	12/8/1987	89	186.5	16	1.97%	8
Second amnesty	3/15/1996	6/1/1996	78	359.0	5	2.50%	5
Third amnesty	4/15/2002	6/10/2002	56	276.9	10	1.51%	13
Fourth amnesty	5/4/2009	6/15/2009	42	725.0	1	2.67%	4
NEW MEXICO							
First amnesty	8/15/1985	11/13/1985	90	13.6	59	0.95%	28
Second amnesty	8/16/1999	11/12/1999	88	45.0	40	1.30%	19
Third amnesty	6/7/2010	9/30/2010	115	N/A			
NEW YORK							
First amnesty	11/1/1985	1/31/1986	91	401.3	4	1.76%	12
Second amnesty	11/1/1996	1/31/1997	91	253.4	13	0.73%	34
Third amnesty	11/18/2002	1/31/2003	74	582.7	2	1.38%	17
Fourth amnesty	10/1/2005	3/1/2006	151	349.0	6	0.61%	42
Fifth amnesty	1/15/2010	3/15/2010	59	56.5	34	0.09%	76
NORTH CAROLINA	9/1/1989	12/1/1989	91	37.6	44	0.51%	46
NORTH DAKOTA							
First amnesty	9/1/1983	11/30/1983	90	0.2	92	0.04%	85
Second amnesty	10/1/2003	1/31/2004	122	6.9	74	0.56%	43
OHIO							
First amnesty	10/15/2001	1/15/2002	92	48.5	38	0.24%	63
Second amnesty	1/1/2006	2/15/2006	45	63.0	33	0.25%	62
OKLAHOMA							
First amnesty	7/1/1984	12/31/1984	183	13.9	58	0.52%	45
Second amnesty	8/15/2002	11/15/2002	92	N/A			
Third amnesty	9/15/2008	11/14/2008	60	81.0	28	0.97%	27
OREGON	10/1/2009	11/19/2009	49	N/A			
PENNSYLVANIA							
First amnesty	10/13/1995	1/10/1996	89	N/A			
Second amnesty	4/26/2010	6/18/2010	53	261.0	11	0.87%	30
RHODE ISLAND							
First amnesty	10/15/1986	1/12/1987	89	0.7	86	0.07%	80
Second amnesty	4/15/1996	6/28/1996	74	7.9	70	0.51%	47
Third amnesty	7/15/2006	9/30/2006	77	6.5	75	0.24%	65
Fourth amnesty	9/2/2012	11/15/2012	74	N/A			
SOUTH CAROLINA							
First amnesty	9/1/1985	11/30/1985	90	7.1	73	0.26%	60
Second amnesty	10/15/2002	12/2/2002	48	66.2	32	1.09%	24
SOUTH DAKOTA	4/1/1999	5/15/1999	44	0.5	88	0.06%	82

(continued)

Table 5.3. *(Continued)*

Name of State (1)	Amnesty Period Begin (2)	Amnesty Period End (3)	Days (4)	Amnesty Collection in current $ (Million) (5)	Rank (6)	Percent of State Total Tax Revenue (7)	Rank (8)
TEXAS							
First amnesty	2/1/1984	2/29/1984	28	0.5	89	0.01%	91
Second amnesty	3/11/2004	3/31/2004	20	N/A			
Third amnesty	6/15/2007	8/15/2007	61	100.0	23	0.25%	61
Fourth amnesty	6/12/2012	8/17/2012	66	100.0	24		
VERMONT							
First amnesty	5/15/1990	6/25/1990	41	1.0	84	0.15%	71
Second amnesty	7/20/2009	8/31/2009	42	2.2	79	0.09%	77
VIRGINIA							
First amnesty	2/1/1990	3/31/1990	58	32.2	48	0.49%	48
Second amnesty	9/2/2003	11/3/2003	62	98.3	25	0.76%	33
Third amnesty	10/7/2009	12/5/2009	59	102.1	20	0.61%	41
WASHINGTON	2/1/2011	4/30/2011	88	320.7	7	1.84%	11
WEST VIRGINIA							
First amnesty	10/1/1986	12/31/1986	91	15.9	56	0.86%	31
Second amnesty	9/1/2004	10/31/2004	60	10.4	65	0.28%	57
WISCONSIN							
First amnesty	9/15/1985	11/22/1985	68	27.3	52	0.54%	44
Second amnesty	6/15/1998	8/14/1998	60	30.9	50	0.28%	59
AVERAGE			76	88.8		0.74%	

Source: FTA, September 2012. *http://www.taxadmin.org/fta/rate/amnesty1.pdf.*
            Web access date: February 17, 2013.

NOTE

1. An alternative to a formal state tax amnesty program is a voluntary disclosure agreement (VDA) which allows taxpayers to file taxes owed from previous years within a binding agreement.

6

A Review of Experience with the
Colorado 1985 Tax Amnesty

The proposition that states are more likely to enact tax amnesties when they are expected to generate a higher tax revenue yield was first advanced by Dubin, Graetz, and Wilde (1992). In examining the 1985 amnesty in Colorado, Alm, and Beck (1993) concluded that tax amnesties were unlikely to have negative effects on long-run tax compliance. These studies together imply that tax amnesties tend to generate a higher tax revenue yield without any overall negative consequences on future tax payer compliance. The apparently misleading implication of these studies may have influenced policies of US states in recent years. Thus, to get to the bottom of these misleading sources and fix them, this chapter focuses on the analysis of 1985 amnesty experience of the State of Colorado to highlight a new and alternative interpretation of the research results. The next chapter (chapter 7) will provide a critique on Dubin, Graetz, and Wilde's 1992 paper.

In 1985, the state of Colorado ran its first tax amnesty program between September 15 and November 15 (Alm 1998, and Alm and Beck 1993). The amnesty was part of a larger, on-going "Colorado Fair Share" initiative aimed at detecting tax evasion and at promoting voluntary tax compliance. The tax amnesty program was authorized by the Legislature and *"Don't Say We Didn't Warn You"* was the main advertising slogan of the program. The amnesty was designed to be a onetime opportunity for individuals as well as businesses to pay any unpaid or underpaid taxes without financial penalties or criminal prosecution.

Taxes offered in the amnesty were as follows: individual income, corporate income, sales, use, gross ton mile, special fuel, cigarette, and liquor taxes. Installment payments were allowed as a method to pay taxes and penalties levied to encourage participation. Although taxpayers who had received notices or billings for back taxes from the federal Internal Revenue Service were eligible for the amnesty, those taxpayers who had received notices or billings from the Colorado tax department were not allowed to participate. Post-amnesty, penalties for tax evasion were increased as were state expenses for people and other resources devoted to tax law enforcement. The amnesty was expected to collect $5 million in tax revenue however actual collections exceeded $6.3 million. Individual income taxes were the largest source of amnesty tax revenues and accounted for over 90 percent of the amnesty collection amount (Alm and Beck 1993).

EMPIRICAL ANALYSIS AND RESULTS

For their data analysis, Alm and Beck (1993) used various time series methods that were expected to perform better than other structural models to predict future movements of a variable (individual income tax). While other methods predict future movements of a variable by relating it to a set of variables in a causal or structural framework, time series methods use the past observations of the same variable to make a prediction or a forecast. In fact, the time series methods extract predictable movements of a variable from its own past observed data and use this information to forecast its future movements. The justification provided by Alm and Beck (1993) to use time series models include (i) difficulty in specifying the precise form of a complete structural model; (ii) unavailability of past data for all structural variables believed to affect the variable of interest (individual income tax); (iii) inability of the structural model to produce accurate standard errors of forecast adversely affecting the forecasted results; (iv) infeasibility of making forecast due to difficulty in obtaining the future values of the structural variables; and, (v) equivalency of a time series equation, when used as a reduced form equation, to that of a complete structural form counterpart (due to Zellner and Palm 1974). Although I agree with their arguments above and their subsequent data analysis, I disagree with them over their research design. If a study begins with a weak research design, its output results are usually invalid. In order to test Alm and Beck's (1993) claim, I complement their research design with data analysis using OLS models with a functional form of semi-log time trend and dummy variables.[1]

For Colorado, I collected quarterly data on individual income tax revenue from the first quarter of 1980 to the fourth quarter of 1989. Data include amnesty revenues over the relevant time period. Table 6.1 presents descriptions of variables along with data sources and summary statistics. We started with the simple analysis of the semi-log time trend model and then continued to a model by entering two dummy variables.

RESULTS FROM SEMI-LOG TIME TREND ANALYSIS

The choice between a linear time-trend model and a growth rate time-trend model depends on whether one is interested in the absolute or relative change in taxes, although for comparative purposes it is the relative change (in taxes) that is generally more important (Gujarati 2003). Alm and Beck (1993) had estimated a linear time-trend model. To complement their analysis, I estimated a semi-log, linear time-trend model of the form:

$$ln(Y_t) = b_0 + b_1 T_t + u_t \qquad (1)$$

Table 6.1. Variable Description and Summary Statistics

Variable Name (source)	Description	No of Observations	Mean	Standard Deviation	Min	Max
Individual Income Tax (1)	Log of state level quarterly individual income tax revenue	40	12.167	0.534	10.371	12.899
Short-run Effect of Amnesty (2)	Equals 1 during the quarter of amnesty, 0 before or after	40	0.05	0.220	0	1
Long-run effect of Amnesty (2)	Equals 1 during and after the quarter of amnesty, 0 before	40	0.45	.503	0	1

1. U.S. Census Bureau, *State Government Finances*, Washington, D.C.
2. Federation of Tax Administrators, *http://www.taxadmin.org/ffta/rate/amnesty1.html*

where $ln(Y_t)$ represents natural log of individual income tax revenue, T_t is the time variable which varies from 1 for the first quarter of 1980 to 40 for the fourth quarter of 1989, u_t is the error term and follows b_0 and b_1 are the OLS parameters. Equation (1) is called a semi-log model because only one variable, tax revenue (the regressand), appears in the logarithmic form. We estimate this equation over the entire period and over the two sub periods before and after amnesty time periods separately. The results are presented in table 6.2.

If the growth rate of state tax collections after the amnesty period changed from before it, then one should be able to detect some statistically significant change in either the parameter of intercept or the slope. In order to test this, I performed the Chow (1960) test for the two sub-periods before and after the amnesty. The results indicated that there was no difference in the two regressions (F-statistics = 1.37). Thus, the growth rate of state individual income tax collections did not change over time.

Next, I introduced the amnesty variable and ran the same regression procedure. The results for this equation are also presented in table 6.2 and I found that the coefficient of the amnesty variable was positive but not statistically significant. I also used a model that included another amnesty related variable. This was an interaction term between time and the amnesty variable. It was obtained by multiplying the time variable with the amnesty variable ($A \times T$). This specification allowed for a different intercept or change in the slope from the amnesty variable. Again, I found that the coefficient of $A \times T$ variable was positive but not statistically significant. Overall, these results confirm that Colorado amnesty did not have any impact on the growth rate of state individual income tax collections and this finding was consistent with the previous findings in the literature.

Table 6.2. Semi-log Time Trend Results (Log of Individual Income Tax as Dependent Variable)

Period	No of Observations	Constant	Time	Amnesty	Amnesty × Time	R^2
1st qtr 1980 – 4th qtr 1989	40	11.44** (102.79)	0.03** (7.45)	-	-	0.59
1st qtr 1980 – 2nd qtr 1985	22	11.31** (57.05)	0.04** (3.12)	-	-	0.32
3rd qtr 1985 – 4th qtr 1989	18	11.80** (59.83)	.02** (3.78)	-	-	0.47
1st qtr 1980 – 4th qtr 1989	40	11.43** (102.24)	0.03** (7.36)	0.22 (0.88)	-	0.60
1st qtr 1980 – 4th qtr 1989	40	11.43** (102.24)	0.03** (7.36)	-	.009 (0.88)	0.60

DUMMY VARIABLES

In the OLS model, I used dummy variables to capture an additive effect of the amnesty on individual income tax revenue. As will be explained in chapter 8, I estimated the impact of offering of a tax amnesty on individual income tax revenue for both short-run and long-run periods. To do so, I included two variables: the first variable captured the short-run effect and was simply a dummy variable equal to one during the third and fourth quarter of 1985 while the amnesty was active. The second variable, to capture the long-run effect, was a dummy variable set to zero prior to the third quarter of 1985 and set to one for every quarter after that. The first of these two variables, the short-run effect, captured any upward spike in tax revenue collections during the quarter when the amnesty was offered. This would be the back taxes collected during the amnesty period. The second, the long-run effect, captured any permanent shift in the revenue collection as measured by the mean of the time series that began with the quarter when the amnesty was offered. This potentially includes two effects. The first effect would be from tax evaders who now come back into the tax system. The second effect would be an increase in the rate of tax evasion as other taxpayers perceived the tax amnesty as a signal of a low cost of switching to tax evasion.

It is of special interest to determine the short-run and long-run impact of 1985 tax amnesty in Colorado. Since the true first period effect was the combined effect of both the short- and long-run coefficients, I entered both variables in the regression model. It was likely that the initial (short run) revenue brought in from overdue taxes would be positive, however, a priori, it was difficult to be sure of the sign of the long-run effect variable. If the dominant effect of the amnesty was to bring tax evaders back into the tax system, then long-run tax revenue would rise. Alternatively, if the dominant effect was to discourage future tax compliance (increasing tax evasion), then tax revenue would fall in the long run. If both effects were present, the long-run effect would be estimated to be close to zero.

Table 6.3 presents the regression results using dummy variables. The results show that the coefficients, on short-run and long-run effects of the amnesty, are not significantly different from zero in both cases. These results further *confirm that the 1985 Colorado amnesty did not have any impact on tax revenues in both the short- or long-run time periods.* Thus, even using alternative models, I arrive at similar conclusion as did Alm and Beck (1993). As I will discuss in detail below, this conclusion suffers from Type II decision error.[2]

DISCUSSION

Except for Alm and Beck (1993), who examined the 1985 Colorado tax amnesty, no study had applied a time-series method to analyze the effects of a state tax amnesty. In this chapter, using quarterly data from individual income tax revenue, I analyzed the short-run and long-run effects of the 1985 Colorado amnesty to test the proposition that the tax amnesty had been successful in raising tax revenues that otherwise would not have been collected. As expected, the re-

Table 6.3.   Simple OLS Results

	Log of Individual Income Tax as Dependent Variable
Constant	11.37***
	(83.50)
Time	0.042***
	(4.27)
Short run effect of amnesty	0.314
	(1.14)
Long run effect of amnesty	-.202
	(0.85)
Number of observations	40
R^2	0.609

Notes: Figures in parenthesis are absolute t-statistics, ***indicates 1 percent significance level.

sults indicated that the Colorado amnesty of 1985 had no short-run or long-run impact on the tax collections and these findings were consistent with the existing literature.

Having established that my results are internally consistent, I am now in a position to explain why the earlier study suffers from Type II decision error. In pioneering, empirical studies on state tax amnesties by Dubin, Graetz, and Wilde (1992), and Alm and Beck (1993), the former authors concluded that states were likely to run tax amnesties when they expected to generate higher yield of tax revenue. The latter authors also found that tax amnesties were unlikely to have any negative effects on long-run tax compliance. Both of these studies implied that amnesties tended to generate higher tax revenues without negative consequences on tax compliance by taxpayers. From a tax policy point of view, these studies could be misconstrued due to (i) the choice of the variables used in both studies; (ii) interpretation of the variables and the assumption used by Dubin, Graetz, and Wilde (1992); and (iii) external validity issue and sample selection bias in Alm and Beck (1993). Chapter 7 will provide a critique of the paper by Dubin, Graetz, and Wilde (1992). Here I discuss only the statistical pitfalls of Alm and Beck's 1993 paper.

Alm and Beck (1993) used personal income tax as a proxy variable for total tax revenue. They claimed that amnesty tax collection from individual income tax was the largest source of taxes in Colorado and it accounted for over 90 percent of the amnesty tax collection.[3] Note that in general, state tax amnesties do not only focus on income taxes. Of the 111 tax amnesties from 1982-2012, ninety-nine included *all major types of state taxes*, and only eleven amnesties were offered for a specific tax, for example income tax, sales tax, and use taxes.[4] Even today, there are several states that do not have income taxes but these states have offered tax amnesties. These states were Florida (1987, 1988, 2003, 2010), Nevada (2002, 2008, 2010), New Hampshire (1997, 2001), South Dakota (1999) and Texas (1984, 2004, 2007, 2012). Let's consider the special case of Texas. Texas does not have a personal income tax and did not have an explicit provision in its state constitution that prohibited imposition of a personal income tax. Following the lead of Connecticut that created a personal income tax in 1991, Texas passed a constitutional amendment in 1993 prohibiting personal income tax (Holcombe 2001). Since then Texas has offered multiple tax amnesties.

It is not uncommon for researchers analyzing the same data to arrive at fundamentally opposite conclusion due largely to the research design employed and methods of data analysis. I used the same descriptive research design and arrived at the same results as did Alm and Beck (1993). In hindsight, I argue that the results on the analysis of taxes collected during the amnesty in Colorado cannot be generalized to a larger population of US states for various reasons. Most importantly, the individual income tax (sample data) from Colorado is not representative because as many as nine out of fifty US states do not have individual income tax at the state level. Although the results of Alm and Beck's (1993) study were internally valid, the authors failed to properly account for the obvious threats to external validity of their findings.[5]

Sample selection bias arises when the availability of data or convenience sample becomes the basis of data selection. Selection of sample data of individual income tax in Alm and Beck's (1993) paper was not based on random sampling rather it was selected on a convenience basis. Thus, the study also suffers from sample selection bias.[6] Note that Alm and Beck (1993) used a subset of tax data from one state amnesty program—1985 amnesty of Colorado—that (sample) was not representative of the larger "population" of taxes collected in other US states (universe). This was another major statistical design weakness of Alm and Beck's 1993 paper. In an examination of short- and long-run revenue effects of an amnesty, pooling data on a large number of state tax amnesties would likely be a more appropriate approach. In retrospect, by not taking into account the basic elements of probability statistics in their research design, Alm and Beck (1993) committed a Type II decision error.

NOTES

1. Ideally I wanted to exactly replicate their results and contacted one of the original authors. But I was not able to obtain the data. It will become clear at the discussion section (pages 38–40) that for my review purpose, the exact replication of Alm and Beck's (1993) results is not necessary.

2. Alm and Beck (1993) do not clearly articulate their null and alternate hypotheses. Below provide them for readers' easier comprehension:

Null hypothesis: an amnesty does not have any effect on tax revenues $(H_0: b_j = 0)$

Alternate hypothesis: an amnesty has an effect on tax revenues $(H_1: b_j \neq 0)$

Alm and Beck (1993) accepted a false null hypothesis of no effect of a tax amnesty on tax revenues where it should have been rejected. This is an example of a Type II decision error.

3. Surprisingly, Alm and Beck's claim could not be independently verified by other researchers (see Mikesell and Ross 2012, table 2).

4. Due to one missing observation, these numbers do not add up to 111. The information for the amnesty North Dakota run between October 1, 2003, and January 31, 2004, was not available.

5. A statistical analysis is internally valid if the statistical inferences about causal effects are valid for the population being studied. The analysis is externally valid if its inferences and conclusions can be generalized from the population and setting studied to other population and settings (Stock and Watson 2003).

6. Sample selection bias is not an inconsequential issue. It often gets ignored for a variety of reasons and, on a side note, we take this opportunity to remind readers of the historical statistical blunder involving sample selection bias in the US. In the general presidential election of 1936, the then Literary Digest magazine embarked on predicting the winner of the election in which the Republican governor of Kansas, Alfred M. Landon, was contending with the then incumbent, President Franklin Delano Roosevelt. According to the *New York Times* article on October 30, 1936, the Literary Digest predicted that Governor Landon would win by an electoral college vote of 370 to 161, would carry 32 of the 48 states, and would lead President Roosevelt about four to three in their share of the popular vote.

When the actual votes were tallied, as Arthur Krock reported in another *New Your Times* article on November 5, 1936, contrary to the Literary Digest's prediction, President Roosevelt won the election by the largest popular and electoral majority—a margin of approximately 11,000,000 plurality of all votes cast, and 523 votes in the electoral college. As a result of the Literary Digest forecasting error, the magazine went bankrupt soon after the 1936 election.

7

A Review of Causes of State Tax Amnesties

"State Income Tax Amnesties: Causes," (hereafter referred to as the previous study) by Dubin, Graetz, and Wilde (1992), cannot be ruled out not to have had an influential role on the public policy debate of state tax amnesties. Based on the assumption of normally distributed hazards, the previous study analyzed the initial wave of state tax amnesties, and concluded that states were likely to run tax amnesties in response to the revenue yield motive.[1] This conclusion was inconsistent with the increased frequency with which states enacted tax amnesties during and after 2001 and 2007-2009 recessions.[2] Thus, the objective of this chapter is to show that the assumption of normally distributed hazards along with several subtle econometric errors that plagued the data analysis in the previous study created a paradox. The results from alternative discrete-time duration models, which take into account the econometric errors in the previous study, unambiguously indicate that the fiscal stress motive, not the revenue yield motive, was the most significant contributing factor leading states to enact amnesties.[3]

DATA

The previous study examined two motives for amnesty adoption by states: revenue yield motive and fiscal stress motive. The revenue yield motive hypothesizes that states enact amnesties when they are most likely to be effective in producing additional tax revenues. The fiscal stress motive hypothesizes that states enact tax amnesties when they are experiencing fiscal stress (e.g., a shortfall in tax revenues, etc.). To point out the inconsistencies in the arguments regarding selection, interpretation and functional forms of variables used for the data analysis in the previous study, I used the same key variables: personal income, tax revenue, and the unemployment rate. The previous study also used the audit rate—defined as the number of individual returns examined by the Internal Revenue Services (IRS) divided by the number of individual returns filed. Since this variable was not statistically significant in all their models, it has not been considered here (also, see *Review of Results from the Previous Study*, below). Here, I describe the similarities and differences in the interpretation of the variables used here and in the previous study.

First, like in the previous study, I used per capita personal income as a measure of a state's fiscal health. The previous study argued a complex relationship between personal income and state tax amnesties due to "(1) direct yield and fiscal stress effects (revenue-based motives for amnesties), (2) filing effects (taxpayers' minimum requirements for filing), and (3) compliance effects (increased opportunities to evade). All these factors except the fiscal stress effect suggest a positive relationship between per capita income and the likelihood of an amnesty" (Dubin, Graetz, and Wilde 1992). Consistent with the fiscal stress hypothesis, I predicted a negative relationship between per capita personal income and the likelihood of a state tax amnesty. Unlike the previous study, I used the per capita income in a natural logarithmic form.

In place of changes in state income tax revenues that the previous study used, I used per capita state total tax revenues as a second measure of fiscal health. If state income tax revenues were used as a measure of state fiscal health, states without income taxes that had enacted amnesties would be ignored from the analysis. It was for this reason, for example, the previous study excluded Texas from the analysis. Note that after Connecticut created a personal income tax in 1991, Texas, which never had a personal income tax, but also did not have an explicit provision in its constitution prohibiting a personal income tax, passed a constitutional amendment prohibiting one in 1993 (Holcombe 2001). Texas has enacted multiple amnesties. There are several other states which do not have income taxes but have enacted amnesties.[4] More importantly, the general state tax amnesties do not focus only on income taxes. Of the 105 amnesties offered during the period of 1982-2010, 95 included all major state taxes, and only ten were for a specific tax (e.g., income tax, sales tax, and use taxes, etc.). Thus, an analysis of a broader measure of tax represented by total tax revenue would be appropriate. I predicted a negative relationship between per capita total tax revenue and the probability that a state introduced an amnesty, consistent with the fiscal stress hypothesis. Since the logarithmic form of a fiscal health variable would capture changes across states and over time through the estimated coefficients, I used the logarithmic form of the total tax revenues. In contrast, the previous study used a change specification of state income tax revenues.[5] Note that for small changes, the first difference of the log of a variable is approximately the same as the percentage change in the variable (Hamilton 1994). Furthermore, economic theory postulates that income and taxes are cointegrated: tax revenues are a function of tax base and tax rate and income can be treated as tax base. If so, the linear combination cancels out the stochastic trends in the log of per capita income and the log of per capita total tax revenues, their entry into the regression models in the levels forms will not produce spurious results (see Engle and Granger 1987). Note, however, that the theory of cointegration itself is subject to criticism (see Moosa 2011, Luitel et al. 2014).

I used the unemployment rate as the final measure of a state's fiscal health but my interpretation of this variable differed from that of the previous study. Regarding the potential relationship between the unemployment rate and state tax amnesties, the previous study put forward a complex argument and yet predicted a positive relationship between these two variables in support of the revenue yield hypothesis. The argument that the presence of per capita income in the regression model should mitigate the effects of unsound economies and that states with high unemployment rates would have greater potential revenue yield from both higher number of non-filers and a larger underground economy was a moot point, because, according to NASBO (2004), states in need of revenues were particularly prone to finding new revenue sources. To the extent that the high unemployment rate in a state also reflected the revenue need of the state, I predicted a positive relationship between the unemployment rate and the probability of a tax amnesty enactment, consistent with the fiscal stress hypothesis. Unlike in the previous study, I used the unemployment rate in a natural logarithmic form. Table 7.1 summarizes the similarities and differences in the arguments regarding selection, interpretation and functional forms of variables as well as other important econometric

Table 7.1. A Comparative Summary of Variables and Descriptive Research Design Employed in the Previous Study and in the Present Study

Previous Study:	Present Study:
1. Uses per capita personal income in level form	1. Uses the log of per capita personal income
2. Uses percentage change in state income tax revenues	2. Uses logs of per capita total state tax revenues
3. Uses the unemployment rate	3. Uses the log of unemployment rate, however, the interpretation is different than used in the previous study.
4. Includes IRS audit rates	4. Does not include IRS audit rates as this variable was not always statistically significant in the previous study and for this reason, it was decided to be inappropriate
5. Purposefully excludes several states from the analysis that enacted tax amnesties during the sample period (i.e. includes only 40 states).	5. Includes all state tax amnesties during the sample period (includes all 50 states).
6. Data covers the period 1980-1988	6. Data covers the period 1982-2010
7. Incorrectly mixes variables in level (per capita personal income) and change specification (state income tax revenue) even when an error correction method was not the basis of data analysis.	7. Economic theory postulates that income and taxes are co-integrated because Tax revenues are a function of tax base and tax rate and income can be treated as tax base. Therefore, use of the two variables (per capita personal income and total state tax revenue) in a logarithmic form does not produce spurious results.
8. Overemphasizes the endogeneity problem and thus incorrectly uses a two-stage least square (2SLS) method.	8. Endogeneity problem is recognized. Data analysis is carried out on the basis of weak exogeneity property. In the absence of endogeneity, single equation method produces consistent and efficient estimators.

issues that have effects in the descriptive research design employed in this study and in the previous study.

I obtained a panel of annual data for all fifty states for the period from 1982 to 2010.[6] Note that these variables are highly correlated, an issue to which I refer in the next section.[7]

EMPIRICAL ANALYSIS AND RESULTS

I used various methods of discrete-time duration model to assess the effects of these variables on the amnesty adoption decision by states. Let A_{it} denote the amnesty status of state i in period t. Then,

$$A_{it} = \begin{cases} 0...\text{if state i does not enact an amnesty in period t} \\ 1...\text{if state i enacts an amnesty in period t} \end{cases} \quad (1)$$

Within the context of hazard model, I defined the *risk set* as those states that had not yet enacted an amnesty and are therefore at risk of introducing one at each point in time. I also defined the hazard (transition) rate, $h(t)$, as the probability that an event—amnesty—would occur at a particular time in a particular state, given that the state was at risk at that time. More formally, the hazard rate for amnesty at time t was defined as:

$$h(t) = \frac{f(t)}{S(t)} \quad (2)$$

where $f(t)$ is the probability of amnesty adoption by states during the interval from t to $t + 1$ and $S(t)$ was the survival function or the probability of not having adopted an amnesty prior to t. Although the hazard rate is unobserved, it controls both the occurrence and the timing of an amnesty; thus, it is the fundamental dependent variable. I modeled this hazard rate as a function of time and other covariates.

Since my objective is to show how alternative discrete-time duration models lead to opposite conclusion, I begin with the review of results from the previous study, and explain inconsistencies in those results, followed by the discussion of results from: (i) Exponential model; (ii) Gompertz model; (iii) Weibull model; and, (iv) Cox model.

Review of Results from the Previous Study

Based on the assumption of normally distributed hazards, the previous study analyzed state tax amnesties in the 1980s. Is normally distributed of hazards a reasonable assumption to analyze the increased frequency of amnesties enacted during and after the 2001 and 2007-2009 recessions? Or, was it valid only for amnesties in the 1980s? To address these questions, I review the previous study, and with hindsight, I point out inconsistencies in the previous study's results.

First, to estimate the parameters, the previous study used a two-stage instrumental variable (2SIV) technique making an argument that the duration model was potentially endogenous to the IRS audit rate. As noted earlier, this variable was not statistically significant in all their models. This was one piece of evidence which gave rise to suspect the conclusion the previous study reached. Although I recognize that the true endogeneity between taxes and amnesty cannot be avoided, estimation and statistical testing can still be performed based on the weak exogeneity property of the data (see Cuthbertson, Hall, and Taylor 1992, Kennedy 2003). Rossana and Seater (1995) showed that the properties of annual data can have very different characteristics from monthly or quarterly data. Engle, Hendry, and Richard (1983) define weak exogeneity, structural invariance, and super exogeneity. These properties are affected by temporal aggregation (Wei 1982, Granger 1990, Marcellino 1999).[8] In a closely related econometric issue of causality, Marcellino (1999) argues that Granger causality may be created or lost due to temporal aggregation.[9] These facts allude to the direction that endogeneity may also be affected by temporal aggregation. This issue is particularly important between taxes and amnesty because a majority of state amnesty programs were approved by legislative authorization and there was generally a significant time lag between the announcement and participation in the amnesty program.[10] Note that in the absence of the statistical endogeneity in the sample data, the coefficient estimates obtained from a single equation method (not from 2SIV) are consistent and efficient.

Second, in the previous study, the duration involved was number of years after 1980 that it took for a state to start an amnesty program. This is problematic since 1980 is an arbitrary starting point because the first amnesty in the previous study's sample started a year later. According to the previous study, Illinois had its first amnesty from December 28, 1981, to January 8, 1982. However, FTA does not list 1981 Illinois amnesty. Moreover, the 1981 Illinois amnesty started four days prior to the end of the year and extended until the first week of 1982, therefore, 1982 would still be a reasonable starting point. Thus, to be consistent, I collected data based on FTA list (which excludes the 1981 Illinois amnesty) and used 1982 as the starting date for the duration analysis when Arizona enacted its first amnesty. It is important to note that in a sample, the hazard estimation results are sensitive to the date at which the estimation begins. For the discussion on the starting point of the duration analysis, see Allison (1984).

Third, table 7.2 below reproduces table IV of the previous study. The table reports results using a percentage change specification in personal income tax revenue as a measure of state fiscal health. Note that the results were obtained by selectively excluding the following states from the analysis: Alaska, Connecticut, Florida, Nevada, New Hampshire, South Dakota, Tennessee, Texas, Washington, and Wyoming. By excluding these states, the results in the table suffered from loss of information because seven of these ten states have had an amnesty, while five states have had multiple amnesties. Moreover, a closer look at the table shows that the coefficients on the key variables were not statistically significant in all models. Thus, these statistically

Table 7.2.   The Previous Study's Results for Amnesties during 1980–1988 Period

TABLE IV.
Duration Model for Time Waited Before Initiating an Amnesty[a]

Variable	Model 1	Calendar year duration Model 2[b]	Model 3	Fiscal year duration Model 4[b]
Constant	-3.52	-2.31	-3.289	-2.58
	(-3.08)	(-1.80)	(-2.87)	(-2.00)
Unemployment Rate	9.23	10.50	9.09	9.83
	(1.93)	(2.14)	(1.88)	(1.93)
Personal Income Per Capita	0.317	0.176	0.333	0.210
	((1.96)	(0.998)	(2.06)	(1.20)
Percentage Change in Real	0.964	1.092	0.832	0.924
State Income Tax Collections	(1.82)	(2.04)	(1.87)	(2.03)
Individual Audit Rate by IRS	-0.179	-0.677	-0.46	-0.564
	(-0.62)	(-2.00)	(-1.48)	(-1.67)
Log-Likelihood	-77.815	-75.960	-78.189	-77.956

a. Based on subset of 40 states that have a significant state tax program. States excluded are Alaska, Connecticut, Florida, Nevada, New Hampshire, South Dakota, Tennessee, Texas, Washington and Wyoming. *t*-statistics are in parentheses.

b. Estimated using the (2SIV) method.

Source: Dubin, Graetz and Wilde (1992). Copyright © *Quarterly Journal of Economics.* Reproduced with permission.

insignificant results to have any economic significance would be a fallacy due to the ignored effects of the subtle econometric concerns raised here. It will soon become clear in the next few sections that the assumption of normally distributed hazards along with these subtle econometric issues led the previous study to an erroneous conclusion. When the subtle econometric issues discussed here are taken into account, I argue that the assumption of normally distributed hazards would be inappropriate to analyze the amnesty adoption process.

Exponential Model

If we assume failures occur randomly, then survival times follow an exponential distribution. In this assumption, a random failure implies that amnesties (events) occur randomly, with constant hazards that do not depend on time. Constant hazards mean that states do not "age," in the sense that they were no more or less likely to enact an amnesty late in the period of observations than they were at the start. In other words, states were equally likely to enact an amnesty in 1982 as they were in 2003 or 2009. I used the exponential model as first approximation for comparison purposes. Mathematically and computationally attractive, the exponential model takes the following form:

$$h(t) = \exp(a + b_j x_j) \tag{3}$$

or,

$$\ln h(t) = a + b_j x_j \tag{4}$$

The results from equation (4) of the exponential model are reported in column (1) of table 7.3 and table 7.4 for the initial and the repeated amnesties. In order to determine the exponential model's goodness of fit, I performed an analysis of pseudo residuals or generalized residuals in the sense of Cox and Snell (1968).[11] If the model fits the data, these residuals should follow a standard exponential distribution. I obtained the generalized Cox-Snell residuals from model (1) of table 7.3 and table 7.4, calculated an empirical estimate of the cumulative hazard function, and plotted it against the Cox-Snell residuals. The results from this exercise are presented in figure 7.1.

Table 7.3. Regression Results for the Initial Amnesties

Variables	Exponential Model (1)	Gompertz Model (2)	Weibull Model (3)	Cox Model (4)
Log of Per capita personal income	-2.325* (2.29)	-4.890** (3.95)	-5.228** (4.51)	-4.169** (3.47)
Log of Per capita total tax revenue	-0.785 (1.20)	-0.827 (1.14)	-0.982 (1.32)	-0.866 (1.23)
Log of Unemployment rate	1.230** (2.64)	1.017* (2.27)	1.542** (3.40)	1.150* (2.28)
Constant	28.254** (3.86)	53.035** (5.33)	57.568** (6.12)	–
LR χ^2 value	$\chi^2_{(3)} =$ 41.76	$\chi^2_{(3)} =$ 59.39	$\chi^2_{(3)} =$ 69.34	$\chi^2_{(3)} =$ 49.43
Probability	0.000	0.000	0.000	0.000
Log likelihood	-158.351	-149.452	-144.117	-218.385
No of observations	559	559	559	559

Notes: Figures in parenthesis are absolute z-statistics. **indicates 1 percent significance level, *indicates 5 percent significance level.

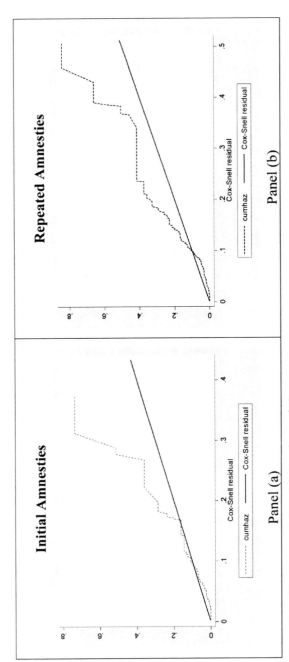

Figure 7.1. The Exponential Model: Goodness of Fit

In the figure, panel (a) corresponds to the initial amnesties, while panel (b) corresponds to the repeated amnesties. As can be seen in the figure, the residual plots revealed substantial departures from the hypothesized exponential model for both the initial amnesties and the repeated amnesties suggesting that the assumption of constant hazards was incorrect. Since many amnesties clustered around different points in time, I did not find any support for the assumption of constant hazards.

Gompertz Model

Next, I relax the assumption of a constant hazard. I then run the Gompertz model, which allows the log of hazards to change linearly with time and takes the following form:

$$\ln h(t) = a + b_j x_j + ct \qquad (5)$$

where c is a constant which may be either positive or negative (Allison 1984). Note that in this model, the transition rate either increases or decreases monotonically with time until an amnesty takes place, but the rate does not change direction.

Table 7.4. Regression Results for the Repeated Amnesties

Variables	Exponential Model (1)	Gompertz Model (2)	Weibull Model (3)	Cox Model (4)
Log of Per capita personal income	0.448 (0.78)	-2.834** (3.99)	-1.883* (2.82)	-2.298** (3.28)
Log of Per capita total tax revenue	-1.303** (2.94)	-1.613** (3.41)	-1.616** (3.41)	-1.296* (-2.85)
Log of Unemployment rate	1.195** (4.43)	0.429 (1.58)	0.930** (3.49)	0.048 (0.16)
Constant	3.434 (0.74)	35.266** (5.45)	25.338** (4.24)	–
LR x^2 value	$x^2_{(3)} =$ 33.48	$x^2_{(3)} =$ 64.13	$x^2_{(3)} =$ 58.15	$x^2_{(3)} =$ 41.13
Probability	0.000	0.000	0.000	0.000
Log likelihood	-417.767	-351.728	-376.053	-703.258
No of observations	1450	1450	1450	1450

Notes: Figures in parenthesis are absolute z-statistics, **indicates 1 percent significance level, *indicates 5 percent significance level.

The results from the Gompertz model are reported in column (2) of table 7.3 and table 7.4. I repeated the analysis of pseudo residuals to assess the goodness of fit of the Gompertz models. As in the exponential model, I obtained the generalized Cox-Snell residuals, calculated an empirical estimate of the cumulative hazard function, and then plotted it against the Cox-Snell residuals. Figure 7.2 shows the results of the Gompertz model where panel (a) corresponds to the initial amnesties, while panel (b) corresponds to the repeated amnesties. Unlike the residual plots in figure 7.1 for the exponential model, the residual plots in figure 7.2 do not show a large departure from the hypothesized Gompertz model for both the initial amnesties and the repeated amnesties.

Weibull Model

Alternatively, I used the Weibull model, which assumes that the log of hazards changes linearly with the log of time and takes the following form:

$$\ln h(t) = a + b_j x_j + c \ln t \tag{6}$$

where c is constrained to be greater than -1 (Allison 1984). Similar to the Gompertz model, in the Weibull model, the transition rate either increases or decreases monotonically with time until an amnesty takes place, but the rate does not change direction.

The results from the Weibull model are reported in column (3) of table 7.3 and table 7.4. I repeated the analysis of pseudo residuals to assess the goodness of fit of the Weibull model. As in the previous two models, I obtained the generalized Cox-Snell residuals, calculated an empirical estimate of the cumulative hazard function, and then plotted it against the Cox-Snell residuals. Figure 7.3 shows the results from the Weibull model. In the figure, panel (a) corresponds to the initial amnesties, while panel (b) corresponds to the repeated amnesties. Unlike the residual plots in figure 7.1 and figure 7.2, the residual plots in figure 7.3 better fitted the hypothesized Weibull model for both the initial amnesties and the repeated amnesties.

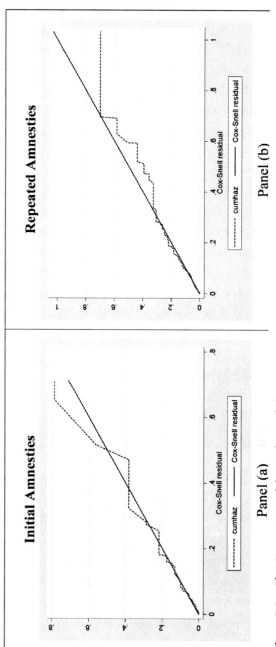

Figure 7.2. The Gompertz Model: Goodness of Fit

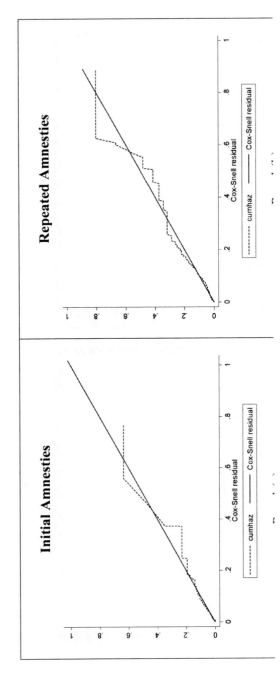

Figure 7.3. The Weibull Model: Goodness of Fit

There are many other models (i.e., logistic, log logistic, log normal, gamma model etc.) that differ only in the way that time enters the equation, but these three models are the most common. While the hazard rate is constant in the exponential model, it may increase or decrease with time, but may not change direction in both the Gompertz and the Weibull models. Thus, a major shortcoming of all three models is that the researcher must assume a constant, increasing, or decreasing relationship between the hazard rate and time, and there is little information on which to base such a choice. More importantly, it is possible that the hazard function is non-monotonic due to co-existence of revenue yield or fiscal stress motives depending on a state's economic condition. For example, if the fiscal stress hypothesis holds, then the hazard function may increase during recessions and decrease during economic expansions. In contrast, if the revenue yield hypothesis holds, the function may decrease during recessions and increase during economic expansions. An intermediate case is also possible where some states enact amnesties in response to fiscal pressure concerns, while others enact them in response to revenue yield concerns. If the hazard function is truly non-monotonic, then none of the above models is appropriate. These shortcomings are overcome in the Cox regression model, which I describe next.

Cox Model

I use Cox's regression model since it does not require any assumption of the relationship between time and the hazard rate. The Cox model is the most general form of the regression models, and takes the following form:

$$h(t,x) = h_0(t)\exp(b_j x_j) \tag{7}$$

where $h(t,...)$ denotes the hazard rate, given the values of the j covariates and the survival time (t). The term $h_0(t)$ denotes the *baseline hazard*, that is, the hazard for each state when the values of all covariates are equal to zero. In this model, the hazard rate is a product of two terms, the first being the baseline hazard rate, $h_0(t)$, and a second specifying the possible influences of the covariates on the transition rate. Dividing both sides of equation (7) by $h_0(t)$ and then taking the natural logarithm of both sides, the model is transformed into a linear form:

$$\ln[\{h(t,x)\}/h_0(t)] = b_j x_j \tag{8}$$

Because this function does not have to be specified, the Cox model is also called partially parametric or semi-parametric, and is often referred to as the "proportional hazards model." Above all, the Cox model is so general and nonrestrictive that it is often considered a satisfactory approximation, even when the proportional hazards assumption is violated (Allison 1984).

Consider the regression results in table 7.3 and table 7.4. The results reveal that not all fiscal health indicators are statistically significant in all models. These results are due to the multicollinearity problem as noted in the previous section. One popular method of addressing the multicollinearity problem is to simply omit one of the collinear variables. However, omitting any one of the key fiscal health indicators from a regression model may lead to the omitted variable bias if the fiscal health indicators are capturing different aspects of the fiscal health of a state.

To give an example of what the numbers in the tables mean, using the Cox model, column (4), results in table 7.3 or table 7.4, a 1 percent increase in per capita income lowers the hazard rate, depending on the model chosen, roughly between 2 and 4 percent. This effect may be easier to understand in relation to average per capita personal income. In the sample, average per capita real personal income is $28,939 in 2005 constant dollars. The results imply that a 1 percent increase in average per capita personal income (from $28,939 to $29,228) lowers the hazard rate by approximately between 2 and 4 percent. Similarly, using the Cox regression model, column (4), results in table 7.3, if a state experiences a 1 percent increase in the unemployment rate, that state's hazard rate increases by approximately

1 percent relative to a state without a change in its unemployment rate. More reasonably, when a state hits hard times, to some extent all three variables might change simultaneously. Thus, states may be more likely to enact amnesties when a decline in income results in lower total tax revenue collections due to rising unemployment rate, which supports the fiscal stress hypothesis.

CONCLUSION

The frequency of tax amnesties increased substantially in the early 2000s with several states offering repeated amnesties. In this chapter, I reexamined whether state tax amnesties were primarily driven by the revenue yield motive or the fiscal stress motive. I used several approaches to event history analyses to investigate the validity of various assumptions regarding the distribution of hazards that could possibly play a role in tax amnesty enactments. Using a Cox regression model, which did not require any assumption about the distribution of hazards, I found a negative relationship between a state's fiscal health and amnesty enactment. The results suggested that fiscal pressures, especially declines in per capita income and per capita state total tax revenue, and increases in the unemployment rate, played an important role in the amnesty adoption decision. These findings are in contrast with the previous study which investigated amnesties in the 1980s and found evidence that states enacted tax amnesties due to a revenue yield motive rather than a fiscal stress motive.

NOTES

1. LeBorgne (2006) points out reasons for possible violation of normally distributed hazards, but he does not go far enough to criticize the previous study.

2. For detail listing of state tax amnesties, see Federation of Tax Administrators (FTA), http://www.taxadmin.org/fta/rate/amnesty1.html

For a discussion of the incentives of state tax amnesties, see National Association of State Budget Officers [NASBO] (2004).

3. Luitel and Tosun (2013) presented an analysis of what motivates states to enact tax amnesties on a repeated basis. This chapter complements Luitel and Tosun (2013).

4. For example, Florida (1987, 1988, 2003, 2010), Nevada (2002, 2008, 2010), New Hampshire (1997, 2001), and South Dakota (1999).

5. In time series analysis, the logic of using a variable in change specification can be traced to the practice of making a series stationary when it has to be differenced. However, this practice is questionable. Harvey (1997) argues that although traditional time series analysis emphasizes the need for differencing a non-stationary time series, it is not always necessary to difference in order to specify a suitable model.

6. Data were collected from the following sources: amnesty—FTA (see note 2 above); personal income—United States Department of Commerce, Bureau of Economic Analysis, *State and Local Area Personal Income,* Washington, D.C.; total tax revenue—United States Census Bureau, *State Government Finances,* Washington, D.C.; unemployment rate—United States Department of Labor, Bureau of Labor Statistics, *Demographics,* Washington, D.C.

7. Untabulated correlation coefficients among the fiscal health variables range from -0.382 between per capita personal income and the unemployment rate to 0.691 between per capita personal income and per capita total tax revenue.

8. To investigate if bidirectional causality between taxes and amnesty creates a problem, I performed Granger causality tests with the log of per capita state total tax revenue and amnesty as bivariate causality models. The test results rejected the presence of causality in the sample data.

9. For the effects of temporal aggregation on (i) consumption, see Ermini (1989); (ii) real wages, see Rossana and Seater (1992); (iii) monetary stocks, see Cunningham and Hardouvelis (1992).

10. The source of sample for this study is FTA list (see note 2 above), according to which, 87 of 105 amnesties were approved by legislative authorization between 1982 and 2010.

11. Although this is an informal method of specification checking, residual plots can reveal departures from a hypothesized model. See Kiefer (1988).

8

Effects of Tax Amnesties on Tax Revenue

Tax revenue (y_t) is a function of tax base (B) and tax rate (t). This simple functional relationship can be expressed as:

$$y_t = f(B, t) \qquad (1)$$

Because my goal is to capture the impact of an amnesty (A) on tax revenue, the relationship can be modified as follows:

$$y_t = f(B, t, A) \qquad (2)$$

An increase (decrease) in tax base increases (decreases) tax revenue; therefore, tax base has a positive effect on tax revenue. The effect of tax rate on tax revenue is ambiguous due to the income and substitution effect. As tax rate increases, so does the gain from evasion on the margin, therefore, tax evasion increases implying that tax revenue decreases—the substitution effect. On the other hand, tax evasion is a risky affair and if caught tax authorities not only confiscate the amount of taxes evaded but also impose additional penalties as a deterrent of breaching the tax rule, which makes tax payers feel poorer than in the situation without tax evasion and lower tax rate. In the special case of decreasing absolute risk aversion, this tends to reduce evasion implying that tax revenue increases—the income effect. Therefore, the net effect of an increase in tax rate on tax revenue is ambiguous.

Furthermore, there is also a Laffer curve argument, that is, if existing tax rate is already high, a further increase in the tax rate decreases tax revenue—that is, the substitution effect dominates; however if existing tax rate is low, then an increase in the tax rate results in an increase in tax revenue—that is, the income effect dominates. Therefore, it is not possible to determine the impact of a change in tax rate on tax revenue.

The key variables of interest—the amnesty variables—capture the impact of offering a tax amnesty on real tax revenue, in both the short run and long run. To do this I include two variables separately for each amnesty offered. The first captures the short-run effect, and is simply a dummy variable equal to one only during the period for which the amnesty is active (which can be one or more quarters). More generally, it can be defined as below: Let A_{it} denote the amnesty status of state i in period t. Then,

$$SA_{it} = \begin{array}{l} 0 \text{ if state } i \text{ does not have an amnesty in period } t \\ \\ 1 \text{ if state } i \text{ enacts an amnesty in period } t \end{array} \qquad (3)$$

This variable captures any upward spike in the revenue collections during the period the amnesty is offered. This would be the revenue generated from the collection of back taxes during the amnesty. The second, to capture the long-run effect, is a dummy variable equal to zero prior to the offering of the tax amnesty and one for every period after the amnesty is offered, forever. More generally, it can be defined as below:

$$LA_{it} = \begin{array}{l} 0 \text{ prior to state } i \text{ enacts an amnesty in period } t \\ \\ 1 \text{ during and after state } i \text{ enacts an amnesty in period } t \end{array} \qquad (4)$$

This variable captures any permanent shift in the mean of the series that begins with the date the amnesty is offered. This potentially includes two effects, the first being the evaders who now come back into the tax system, permanently increasing revenue, and the second being an increase in tax evasion as other taxpayers see the offering of the amnesty as a sign of a low cost of switching to tax evasion. Note, however, that the true first period effect is the combined effect of both the short- and long-run coefficients.

The above theoretical framework provides a basis for the following empirical specification:

$$y_{it} = \beta_0 + \beta_{1j}A_j + \beta_{2j}x_{jit} + \beta_{3j}z_{jit} + f_i + \phi_t + \varepsilon_t \qquad (5)$$

where y_{it} denotes tax revenue for state i in period t, A_j denotes short-run and long-run effects of amnesty, x_{jit} denotes explanatory variables of tax revenue such as personal income and tax rates. z_{jit} denotes other control variables such as population and unemployment rate. f_i represents the unobservable state specific, time-invariant effects, ϕ_t represents unobservable time specific effects. Finally, ε_t represents white noise, that is, time-variant unsystematic effects and is i.i.d. Thus, I use state dummies and time dummies to control for these state specific and time specific effects.[1]

I use two measures of tax revenue: total tax revenue and per capita total tax revenue. When per capita total state tax revenue is the dependent variable, relevant explanatory variables are also used in per capita terms and population is dropped from the regression. All variables except dummies are entered in logarithmic form. I obtain a panel of quarterly tax data for all fifty states over the 1980–2004 periods. Descriptions of the variables, data sources, and summary statistics are presented in table 8.1. The matrices of correlation coefficients are presented in table 8.2a and table 8.2b. The results of the heteroskedasticity tests are presented in table 8.3.

I start with simple OLS. The regression results are presented in table 8.4. Next, I proceed to run regression diagnostics to check for multicollinearity and heteroskedasticity in the models. No such problems are detected. Since my technique involves many different dummy variables, I perform a sensitivity analysis by running specifications on important subsets of the data. In particular, I estimate the model on subsets of the data based on the number of amnesties offered by the state. I estimate the regression only among states with zero or one amnesty,

Table 8.1. Variable Description, Data Sources and Summary Statistics

(All data are quarterly, and at the state level)

Variable Name (source)	Description	No of Observation	Mean	Standard Deviation	Minimum	Maximum
Total Tax Revenue (1)	Total real tax revenue	4938	2.04e+09	2.58e+09	7.93e+07	2.84e+10
Total Tax Revenue Per Capita (1)	Total real tax revenue per capita	4938	396.644	170.849	84	3729
Short-run Effect of Amnesty (2)	Equals 1 during period of amnesty, 0 before or after					
Short-run Effect of Amnesty 1 (2)	Equals 1 during period of first amnesty, 0 before or after	5000	0.0134	0.115	0	1
Short-run Effect of Amnesty 2 (2)	Equals 1 during period of second amnesty, 0 before or after	5000	0.010	0.100	0	1
Short-run Effect of Amnesty 3 (2)	Equals 1 during period of third amnesty, 0 before or after	5000	0.003	0.051	0	1
Long-run Effect of Amnesty 1 (2)	Equals 1 during and after period of first amnesty, 0 before	5000	0.530	0.499	0	1
Long-run Effect of Amnesty 2 (2)	Equals 1 during and after period of second amnesty, 0 before	5000	0.094	0.292	0	1
Long-run Effect of Amnesty 3 (2)	Equals 1 during and after period of third amnesty, 0 before	5000	0.016	0.126	0	1
Average of the Personal Income Tax Rate (3)	Average personal income tax rate	4056	0.059	0.046	0.015	0.280
Average of the Corporate Income Tax Rate (3)	Average corporate income tax rate	4500	0.068	0.019	0.018	0.127
Average of the Sales Tax Rate (3)	Sales tax rate in the state	4500	0.048	0.011	0.02	0.08
Personal Income (4)	Real personal income of residents	5000	1.27e+11	1.55e+11	8.06e+09	1.18e+12
Personal Income Per Capita (4)	Real personal income per capita of residents	5000	23522.85	5046.307	12620	42527
Population (5)	State population	5000	5123928	5571192	401851	3.59e+07
Unemployment rate (6)	State unemployment rate	5000	0.059	0.020	0.021	0.181

1. U.S. Census Bureau, *State Government Finances*. Washington, D.C.
2. Federation of Tax Administrators, *http://www.taxadmin.org/fta/rate/amnesty1.html*
3. Commerce Clearing House, Inc., *State Tax Handbook*. 1980 – 2003.
4. U.S. Department of Commerce, Bureau of Economic Analysis, *State and Local Personal Income*. Washington, D. C.
5. U.S. Census Bureau, *Population Estimates*. Washington, D.C
6. U.S. Department of Labor, Bureau of Labor Statistics, *Demographics*, Washington, D.C.

	Short-run Effect of Amnesty 1	Short-run Effect of Amnesty 2	Short-run Effect of Amnesty 3	Long-run Effect of Amnesty 1	Long-run Effect of Amnesty 2	Long-run Effect of Amnesty 3	Log of Personal Income	Log of Personal Income Tax Rate	Log of Corporate Income Tax Rate	Log of Sales Tax Rate	Log of Population	Log of Unemployment Rate
Short-run Effect of Amnesty 1	1											
Short-run Effect of Amnesty 2	-0.014	1										
Short-run Effect of Amnesty 3	-0.006	0.096	1									
Long-run Effect of Amnesty 1	0.093	0.082	0.037	1								
Long-run Effect of Amnesty 2	-0.040	0.341	0.154	0.240	1							
Long-run Effect of Amnesty 3	-0.017	0.099	0.369	0.099	0.416	1						
Log of Personal Income	-0.009	0.032	0.050	0.167	0.134	0.116	1					
Log of Personal Income Tax Rate	0.008	-0.023	-0.016	0.030	0.036	-0.046	-0.454	1				
Log of Corporate Income Tax Rate	0.007	-0.011	0.019	0.087	0.044	0.046	0.176	0.203	1			
Log of Sales Tax Rate	-0.041	0.034	0.004	0.301	0.099	-0.002	0.113	0.057	0.317	1		
Log of Population	0.002	0.012	0.040	0.080	0.072	0.089	0.980	-0.509	0.121	0.052	1	
Log of Unemployment Rate	0.056	-0.012	0.004	-0.218	-0.037	-0.004	0.036	-0.160	-0.148	-0.061	0.172	1

(continued)

Table 8.2b. Matrix of Correlation Coefficient

	Short-run Effect of Amnesty 1	Short-run Effect of Amnesty 2	Short-run Effect of Amnesty 3	Long-run Effect of Amnesty 1	Long-run Effect of Amnesty 2	Long-run Effect of Amnesty 3	Log of Personal Income Per Capita	Log of Personal Income Tax Rate	Log of Corporate Income Tax Rate	Log of Sales Tax Rate	Log of Unemployment Rate
Short-run Effect of Amnesty 1	1										
Short-run Effect of Amnesty 2	-0.014	1									
Short-run Effect of Amnesty 3	-0.006	0.096	1								
Long-run Effect of Amnesty 1	0.093	0.082	0.037	1							
Long-run Effect of Amnesty 2	-0.040	0.341	0.154	0.240	1						
Long-run Effect of Amnesty 3	-0.017	0.099	0.369	0.099	0.416	1					
Log of Personal Income Per Capita	-0.051	0.098	0.065	0.439	0.320	0.166	1				
Log of Personal Income Tax Rate	0.008	-0.023	-0.016	0.030	0.036	-0.046	0.027	1			
Log of Corporate Income Tax Rate	0.007	-0.011	0.019	0.087	0.044	0.046	0.310	0.203	1		
Log of Sales Tax Rate	-0.041	0.034	0.004	0.301	0.099	-0.002	0.307	0.057	0.316	1	
Log of Unemployment Rate	0.056	-0.012	0.004	-0.218	-0.037	-0.004	-0.554	-0.160	-0.148	-0.061	1

Table 8.3. Results of Breusch-Pagan/Cook-Weisberg Test for Heteroskedasticity

Dependent Variables	χ^2	Probability
Log of total tax revenue	0.04	0.835
Log of per capita total tax revenue	0.56	0.454

Table 8.4. OLS Regression Results

	Dependent Variables					
	Log of Total Tax Revenue			Log of Per Capita Total Tax Revenue		
Variables	States with one Amnesty	States with one & two Amnesties	States with one, two, & three Amnesties	States with one Amnesty	States with one & two Amnesties	States with one, two, & three Amnesties
	(1)	(2)	(3)	(4)	(5)	(6)
Short-run effect of Amnesty1	0.064* (2.17)	0.059** (3.36)	0.047** (3.05)	0.064* (2.18)	0.059** (3.34)	0.047** (3.03)
Short-run effect of Amnesty2	–	-0.009 (0.37)	0.016 (0.88)	–	-0.009 (0.38)	0.017 (0.95)
Short-run effect of Amnesty3	–	–	0.024 (0.58)	–	–	0.020 (0.51)
Long-run effect of Amnesty1	-0.041** (3.17)	-0.035** (4.12)	-0.029** (3.73)	-0.039** (3.04)	-0.036** (4.26)	-0.030** (3.76)
Long-run effect of Amnesty2	–	-0.024* (2.03)	-0.047** (5.03)	–	-0.026* (2.19)	-0.049** (5.24)
Long-run effect of Amnesty3	–	–	-0.008 (0.47)	–	–	-0.011 (0.66)
Log of Personal Income	0.812** (7.15)	0.980** (13.97)	1.011** (16.54)	–	–	–
Log of Per Capita Personal Income	–	–	–	0.778** (7.20)	1.004** (14.54)	1.022** (16.74)
Log of Population	0.117 (0.77)	0.114 (1.25)	0.020 (0.28)	–	–	–
Log of Personal Income Tax Rate	0.009 (0.62)	-0.020 (1.72)	-0.002 (0.18)	0.007 (0.49)	-0.020 (1.68)	-0.001 (0.09)
Log of Corporate Income Tax Rate	0.131** (2.82)	0.021 (0.85)	0.039 (1.80)	0.139** (3.06)	0.009 (0.39)	0.040 (1.83)
Log of Sales Tax Rate	0.201** (5.00)	0.162** (7.30)	0.160** (7.75)	0.197** (4.93)	0.157** (7.13)	0.159** (7.70)
Log of unemployment rate	-0.030 (1.32)	-0.066** (4.59)	-0.069** (5.55)	-0.036 (1.66)	-0.058** (4.21)	-0.066** (5.45)
Constant	-0.282 (0.22)	-5.156** (5.33)	-4.329** (4.95)	-0.879 (0.78)	-3.804** (5.52)	-3.833** (6.32)
R^2	0.987	0.988	0.988	0.877	0.845	0.850
No of Observations	1294	3073	3666	1294	3073	3666

Notes: Figures in parenthesis are absolute t-statistics. **indicates 1 percent significance level. *indicates 5 percent significance level.

then reestimate it expanding the sample to states with two amnesties, then again to states with three amnesties. Although no heteroskedasticity and endogeneity is found to be present in the data, for comparison purposes, I run regressions from GLS and maximum likelihood estimation (MLE) methods. The results are reported in table 8.5 and table 8.6. Finally, because my data set is panel data, I run random effects and fixed effects models. The results of the random effects and fixed effects models are shown in tables 8.7 and table 8.8. The Hausman test statistics, presented in the bottom row of table 8.7, allows me to use random effects model but as there is no significant gain using the random effects model, so I use the fixed effects model.[2]

Comparing columns (1) vs (4), (2) vs (5), and (3) vs (6), it makes little difference whether I use total tax revenue or total tax revenue per capita as the dependent variable—the coefficient estimates of amnesty variables are almost identical. This is true across all regression specifications (i.e., OLS, GLS, fixed effects, random effects, and maximum likelihood estimation methods). Next, comparing the first three columns in table 8.8, again the results are robust to whether I include or exclude states that have offered multiple amnesties. I tend to prefer what I consider the most appropriate 'full' model, which appears in column (3) of table 8.8. The estimates from that model are the ones I discuss below.

The significant, positive short-run coefficient estimate for amnesty 1 can be interpreted to suggest that the average impact of offering the first amnesty in a state is between a 4 and 5 percent increase in real tax revenue during the period of the amnesty due to the increased collections of previous evaders.[3] The significant, negative long-run coefficient estimate for amnesty 1 can be interpreted to suggest that the long-run impact of offering this first tax amnesty is significantly negative on revenue, resulting in about a 2 to 3 percent ongoing loss each period after the amnesty due to reduced compliance. In fact, the true first period impact of the amnesty would be the short-run inflow of short-run revenue and also the long-run revenue loss combined. After the first period, only the

Table 8.5. GLS Regression Results

	Dependent Variables					
	Log of Total Tax Revenue			Log of Per Capita Total Tax Revenue		
Variables	States with one Amnesty	States with one & two Amnesties	States with one, two, & three Amnesties	States with one Amnesty	States with one & two Amnesties	States with one, two, & three Amnesties
	(1)	(2)	(3)	(4)	(5)	(6)
Short-run effect of Amnesty1	0.064* (2.28)	0.059** (3.44)	0.048** (3.11)	0.064* (2.29)	0.059** (3.42)	0.047** (3.09)
Short-run effect of Amnesty2	–	-0.009 (0.38)	0.016 (0.90)	–	-0.009 (0.39)	0.017 (0.97)
Short-run effect of Amnesty3	–	–	0.024 (0.59)	–	–	0.020 (0.52)
Long-run effect of Amnesty1	-0.041** (3.32)	-0.035** (4.22)	-0.029** (3.81)	-0.039** (3.19)	-0.036** (4.36)	-0.030** (3.84)
Long-run effect of Amnesty2	–	-0.024* (2.07)	-0.047** (5.14)	–	-0.026* (2.24)	-0.049** (5.35)
Long-run effect of Amnesty3	–	–	-0.008 (0.48)	–	–	-0.011 (0.67)
Log of Personal Income	0.812** (7.50)	0.980** (14.30)	1.011** (16.88)	–	–	–
Log of Per Capita Personal Income	–	–	–	0.778** (7.55)	1.004** (14.88)	1.022** (17.08)
Log of Population	0.117 (0.81)	0.114 (1.28)	0.020 (0.29)	–	–	–
Log of Personal Income Tax Rate	0.009 (0.65)	-0.020 (1.76)	-0.002 (0.18)	0.007 (0.52)	-0.020 (1.72)	-0.001 (0.10)
Log of Corporate Income Tax Rate	0.131** (2.96)	0.021 (0.87)	0.039 (1.83)	0.139** (3.21)	0.009 (0.40)	0.040 (1.87)
Log of Sales Tax Rate	0.201** (5.25)	0.161** (7.47)	0.161** (7.91)	0.197** (5.17)	0.157** (7.30)	0.159** (7.86)
Log of unemployment rate	-0.030 (1.39)	-0.066** (4.70)	-0.068** (5.67)	-0.036 (1.74)	-0.058** (4.31)	-0.066** (5.56)
Constant	-0.292 (0.22)	-5.156** (5.46)	-4.164** (5.56)	-0.879 (0.82)	-3.804** (5.64)	-3.991** (6.71)
No of Observations	1294	3073	3666	1294	3073	3666

Notes: Figures in parentheses are absolute z-statistics, **indicates 1 percent significance level, *indicates 5 percent significance level.

Table 8.6. Maximum Likelihood Estimation Results

	Dependent Variables					
	Log of Total Tax Revenue			Log of Per Capita Total Tax Revenue		
Variables	States with one Amnesty	States with one & two Amnesties	States with one, two, & three Amnesties	States with one Amnesty	States with one & two Amnesties	States with one, two, & three Amnesties
	(1)	(2)	(3)	(4)	(5)	(6)
Short-run effect of Amnesty1	0.063* (2.24)	0.058* (3.40)	0.047** (3.08)	0.064* (2.27)	0.059** (3.40)	0.047** (3.06)
Short-run effect of Amnesty2	–	-0.009 (0.39)	0.016 (0.92)	–	-0.009 (0.37)	0.018 (0.98)
Short-run effect of Amnesty3	–	–	0.027 (0.66)	–	–	0.020 (0.51)
Long-run effect of Amnesty1	-0.042** (3.43)	-0.035** (4.28)	-0.030** (3.84)	-0.039** (3.22)	-0.035** (4.26)	-0.029** (3.73)
Long-run effect of Amnesty2	–	-0.026* (2.27)	-0.049** (5.37)	–	-0.026* (2.23)	-0.049** (5.37)
Long-run effect of Amnesty3	–	–	-0.012 (0.68)	–	–	-0.012 (0.72)
Log of Personal Income	0.851** (8.20)	0.968** (14.60)	0.972** (16.88)	–	–	–
Log of Per Capita Personal Income	–	–	–	0.793** (7.80)	0.958** (14.57)	0.970** (16.82)
Log of Population	0.064 (0.55)	0.007 (0.09)	-0.004 (0.06)	–	–	–
Log of Personal Income Tax Rate	0.009 (0.69)	-0.017 (1.51)	-0.00007 (0.01)	0.010 (0.73)	-0.016 (1.45)	0.002 (0.23)
Log of Corporate Income Tax Rate	0.125** (2.94)	0.004 (0.15)	0.031 (1.50)	0.132** (3.08)	0.007 (0.30)	0.035 (1.67)
Log of Sales Tax Rate	0.198** (5.21)	0.155** (7.24)	0.155** (7.74)	0.196** (5.16)	0.156** (7.30)	0.156** (7.78)
Log of unemployment rate	-0.028 (1.30)	-0.058** (4.19)	-0.066** (5.45)	-0.036 (1.81)	-0.061** (4.50)	-0.069** (5.77)
Constant	-0.380 (0.34)	-3.096** (4.42)	-2.932** (4.78)	-1.096 (1.03)	-3.366** (5.17)	-3.390** (5.93)
No of Observations	1294	3073	3666	1294	3073	3666

Notes: Figures in parenthesis are absolute z-statistics, **indicates 1 percent significance level, *indicates 5 percent significance level.

Table 8.7. Random Effects Regression Results

Variables	Log of Total Tax Revenue			Log of Per Capita Total Tax Revenue		
	States with one Amnesty	States with one & two Amnesties	States with one, two, & three Amnesties	States with one Amnesty	States with one & two Amnesties	States with one, two, & three Amnesties
	(1)	(2)	(3)	(4)	(5)	(6)
Short-run effect of Amnesty1	0.062* (2.08)	0.059** (3.34)	0.047** (3.04)	0.064* (2.18)	0.059** (3.34)	0.047** (3.02)
Short-run effect of Amnesty2	–	-0.009 (0.38)	0.016 (0.90)	–	-0.009 (0.37)	0.018 (0.96)
Short-run effect of Amnesty3	–	–	0.027 (0.64)	–	–	0.020 (0.50)
Long-run effect of Amnesty1	-0.041** (3.29)	-0.035** (4.21)	-0.030** (3.79)	-0.039** (3.07)	-0.035** (4.20)	-0.029** (3.69)
Long-run effect of Amnesty2	–	-0.026* (2.21)	-0.049** (5.26)	–	-0.026* (2.20)	-0.049** (5.29)
Long-run effect of Amnesty3	–	–	-0.011 (0.64)	–	–	-0.012 (0.70)
Log of Personal Income	0.915** (8.89)	0.975** (14.32)	0.981** (16.68)	–	–	–
Log of Per Capita Personal Income	–	–	–	0.786** (7.37)	0.968** (14.53)	0.977** (16.86)
Log of Population	-0.004 (0.04)	0.014 (0.18)	-0.006 (0.08)	–	–	–
Log of Personal Income Tax Rate	0.009 (0.62)	-0.017 (1.52)	-0.0004 (0.04)	0.009 (0.61)	-0.017 (1.48)	0.002 (0.18)
Log of Corporate Income Tax Rate	0.117** (2.76)	0.006 (0.24)	0.032 (1.52)	0.135** (3.01)	0.008 (0.32)	0.035 (1.67)
Log of Sales Tax Rate	0.188** (4.80)	0.156** (7.12)	0.156** (7.63)	0.197** (4.95)	0.156** (7.17)	0.156** (7.68)
Log of unemployment rate	-0.024 (1.11)	-0.059** (4.19)	-0.066** (5.40)	-0.037 (1.70)	-0.060** (4.38)	-0.068** (5.66)
Constant	-1.021 (0.95)	-3.377** (4.69)	-3.136** (4.91)	-1.019 (0.91)	-3.465** (5.25)	-3.455** (6.02)
R^2	0.967	0.968	0.969	0.618	0.557	0.595
No of Observations	1294	3073	3666	1294	3073	3666
Hausman Test	$\chi^2(107) = 5.30$	$\chi^2(109) = 11.28$	$\chi^2(111) = 7.98$	$\chi^2(106) = 2.06$	$\chi^2(108) = 6.79$	$\chi^2(110) = 9.10$

Dependent Variables

Table 8.8. Fixed Effects Regression Results

	Dependent Variables					
	Log of Total Tax Revenue			Log of Per Capita Total Tax Revenue		
Variables	States with one Amnesty	States with one & two Amnesties	States with one, two, & three Amnesties	States with one Amnesty	States with one & two Amnesties	States with one, two, & three Amnesties
	(1)	(2)	(3)	(4)	(5)	(6)
Short-run effect of Amnesty1	0.064* (2.17)	0.059** (3.36)	0.048** (3.05)	0.064* (2.18)	0.059** (3.34)	0.047** (3.03)
Short-run effect of Amnesty2	-	-0.009 (0.37)	0.016 (0.88)	-	-0.009 (0.38)	0.017 (0.95)
Short-run effect of Amnesty3	-	-	0.025 (0.58)	-	-	0.020 (0.51)
Long-run effect of Amnesty1	-0.041** (3.17)	-0.035** (4.12)	-0.029** (3.73)	-0.039** (3.04)	-0.036** (4.26)	-0.030** (3.76)
Long-run effect of Amnesty2	-	-0.024* (2.03)	-0.047** (5.03)	-	-0.026* (2.19)	-0.049** (5.24)
Long-run effect of Amnesty3	-	-	-0.008 (0.47)	-	-	-0.011 (0.66)
Log of Personal Income	0.812** (7.15)	0.980** (13.97)	1.011** (16.54)	-	-	-
Log of Per Capita Personal Income	-	-	-	0.778** (7.20)	1.004** (14.54)	1.022** (16.74)
Log of Population	0.117 (0.77)	0.114 (1.25)	0.020 (0.28)	-	-	-
Log of Personal Income Tax Rate	0.009 (0.62)	-0.020 (1.72)	-0.002 (0.18)	0.007 (0.49)	-0.020 (1.68)	-0.001 (0.09)
Log of Corporate Income Tax Rate	0.131** (2.82)	0.021 (0.85)	0.039 (1.80)	0.139** (3.06)	0.009 (0.39)	0.040 (1.83)
Log of Sales Tax Rate	0.201** (5.00)	0.162** (7.30)	0.161** (7.75)	0.197** (4.93)	0.157** (7.13)	0.159** (7.70)
Log of unemployment rate	-0.030 (1.32)	-0.066** (4.59)	-0.068** (5.55)	-0.036 (1.66)	-0.058** (4.21)	-0.066** (5.45)
Constant	-0.201 (0.15)	-4.973** (5.60)	-4.278** (5.27)	-0.920 (0.82)	-3.830** (5.62)	-3.903** (6.49)
R^2	0.966	0.967	0.969	0.615	0.551	0.588
No of Observations	1294	3073	3666	1294	3073	3666

Notes: Figures in parenthesis are absolute t-statistics, **indicates 1 percent significance level, *indicates 5 percent significance level.

long-run impact remains. The second amnesty does not produce as much short-run revenue (in fact, the results are insignificantly different from zero), but does produce a significant and negative long-run effect that is greater than the negative long-run effect for the first amnesty. Finally, when a state offers a third amnesty, again there is no significant short-run revenue produced. Though negative, the estimates for the long-run impact of the third amnesty appear insignificant. This may be due to the small number of states for which third amnesty data is available and in the regression.

Based on these results, we can conclude that if a state is considering offering a tax amnesty to raise total tax revenue, the impact *will* depend on whether the state has previously offered an amnesty, and that it will probably never be a good idea at all. On average, first-time tax amnesties do tend to produce a significant 4 to 5 percent increase in revenue during the period the amnesty is being offered. They, however, also tend to discourage compliance to the magnitude of 2 percent per period, from then on. This certainly doesn't seem like a worthwhile tradeoff, without assuming a fantastically large discount rate. The public choice literature, however, is filled with examples of shortsighted political behavior that could be consistent in explaining why states would still adopt an amnesty given these numbers.

On average, if a state has already offered one previous amnesty, and is considering running a second, they will likely see only a small (insignificant) increase in revenue during the amnesty period, followed by a significant, and larger, negative effect on long-run revenue. The third amnesty continues this trend, with little short-run revenue and larger long-run revenue losses. These results are consistent with our expectations, and likely make sense to most tax researchers and practitioners. Tax amnesties are similar to the story of the boy who cried wolf. When they are offered on a repeated basis, they tend to discourage compliance to a greater extent than if they are only offered once. In addition, the revenue boost produced by an amnesty as former evaders pay up their tax liabilities during the amnesty period is significant only the first time a state offers an amnesty. This would suggest that the first amnesty to a great extent brings most evaders back into the system that would be willing to do so, and there is little benefit from repeating the amnesty within a short window of time.

NOTES

1. Because my data set is quarterly, as a matter of fact, I include quarter dummies (quarter 1, quarter 2, quarter 3, quarter 4, quarter 5, quarter 6, ..., quarter N=100).

2. The parameter estimates obtained from fixed effects model are consistent under H_0 and H_a. The parameter estimates obtained from random effects model are inconsistent under H_a but efficient under H_0. I perform the Hausman test of the null hypothesis that the difference in coefficients obtained from both fixed effects and random effects models are not systematic. The test statistics in all cases suggest that we cannot reject the null hypothesis.

3. Because this is a semi-logarithmic equation, a precise percentage effect must be calculated from a dummy variable coefficient as $\% = (e^{\beta}-1)*100$, see Halvorsen and Palmquist (1980). This makes a small difference, as, for example, the 0.046 coefficient translates into a 4.71 percent change.

9

Summary, Discussion and Conclusion

At the turn of the twenty-first century, many states turned to offering tax amnesties as a way to generate additional tax revenue. In many of these cases the amnesty was a second, third, fourth, or even fifth amnesty offered by the state. I examined whether the revenue effects of offering a tax amnesty change as the amnesty is offered on a repeated basis, something that has not been previously examined in the literature. I distinguish between the effect the amnesty has on revenue in the period accompanying the amnesty program (the short-run effect) and the effect the amnesty has on the permanent mean level of tax revenue (the long-run effect). The results indicate that overall, when a state offers an amnesty for the first time, it seems to produce a short-run revenue boost during the amnesty period but then leads to a reduction in revenue in the long run, which is consistent with the theory proposing that people respond to the amnesty by beginning to evade taxes in anticipation of additional future amnesties. Repeated broad-based amnesties produce little or no additional short-run revenue, while creating increasing long-run revenue losses due to reduced compliance that grow as additional amnesties are offered.

The controversy surrounding the ability of an amnesty to generate additional short-term tax revenues during the amnesty period arises from several sources. First, not all states report recovery of taxes from an amnesty. Second, even when amnesties were reported to have been successful, recovery of taxes were reported in absolute, gross values, thereby making comparison across states and over time difficult. Third, gross values reported likely did not take into account the cost of tax amnesty administration because the tax amnesty program was administered with resources redirected from existing department. Finally, gross dollar values reported from taxes recovered from an amnesty often ignore the interest and penalties as program costs. Ignoring these costs would exaggerate the amount of taxes recovered from an amnesty (Malik and Schwab 1991, Stella 1991, JCS-2-98 1998, and Mikesell and Ross 2012). Despite these shortcomings, a look at the available raw data on gross tax amnesty collection (table 5.3) shows a large variation in short-term tax revenue yield among states. Twenty-four state tax amnesties were reported to have brought in short-run revenues greater than or equal to $100 million and ten states generated $1 million or less.

As indicated above, absolute dollar amounts collected from tax amnesties were not directly comparable due to differences in state population (e.g., California vs. South Dakota). Moreover, the gross collection figures were not adjusted for inflation. Thus, gross collections in the 1980s were not directly comparable to the collections in the 1990s or 2000s. To some extent, this weakness was overcome by using a percentage calculation, that enabled both cross-state and cross-year comparison (JCS-2-98 1998). Column (7) of table 5.3 shows that between 1982 and 2012, amnesties generated average tax collections of only 0.74 percent, and never more than 3 percent, of total state tax collections. Though not trivial, these amnesty tax collections were relatively small compared to total tax collections in the states. Thus, the ability of a tax amnesty to generate even the short-term tax revenue was not supported by the evidence.

Given that state tax amnesties have become a more commonplace component of state tax administration, what lessons can be learned from state experiences? As reported in the literature, states would likely realize a small, one time, increase in tax revenue during the amnesty period and these short-run gains in tax revenue come at the expense of long-run tax revenue losses due to reduced future tax compliance attributable to the amnesty. Using any reasonable discount rate, even the one time increase in tax revenue during the amnesty period cannot be considered a net gain in total tax revenue once the long-run compliance effects are taken into account. To put the state fiscal policy (regarding tax amnesties) into perspective with the funding cuts and tuition increases in higher education, tax amnesty becomes a "penny wise and a pound foolish" policy that potentially impedes a state's future progress.[1] In a recent study, it was shown that the firms that had their headquarters located in states offering a tax amnesty program were more likely to engage in financial irregularities during or just prior to the amnesty period (Buckwalter et. al. 2013). This unintended consequence of state tax amnesty policy is particularly worrisome because US states keep names of amnesty participants a secret and there is a real danger that these tax amnesties that some authors describe as simply "an asset laundering device," can potentially promote organized racketeering.[2] Ordinary and hardworking American citizens should become mindful of these potential developments in the state tax administration system.

In the time since 1993, when Alm and Beck (1993) first reported on state tax amnesty, more research findings have been reported and we have learned more about the longer term consequences of state tax amnesties. One of the knowledge that we have going back to 1993, is that a state tax amnesty is not tax revenue neutral. I do not recommend this as a sound tax policy because (a) tax amnesties do not collect substantial tax revenues in the short run, and (b) in the long run, they have unintended consequences of taxpayers gaming the tax system in expectation of a pending tax amnesty.

State tax amnesties are nothing more than another example of a policy failure. These amnesties have proved that if the information received by governments for policy formulation is incorrect or of dubious quality, the policy decisions made by government will be equally poor. More recently, the US government shutdown of 2013 has revealed the need to rethink fundamentally not only about the general decline in ethical behavior of the policy makers in the United

States, but also made it abundantly clear that after the 2007-2009 recession, the major American economic journals have once again failed to alert their policy makers about the adverse consequences of such unethical behavior whose real costs have the potential to spill over national boundaries. Disappointingly, however, what has been reported about the academic dishonesty in economics literature and what appears, albeit infrequently, in the public news media is only a tip of the iceberg. How deep the disease of the academic dishonesty is in economics discipline in general and why one should worry about the rise of this disease in the United States in particular is a revealing subject area, which I leave for future research.

NOTES

1. One of the outcomes of state and local government funding cuts to higher education in the USA after the 2001 recession was an increase in state college and university tuition fees and these fees continue to rise at a rate faster than inflation and family incomes. Average published tuition for in-state students at public, four-year colleges and universities increased by over 66 percent from $5,213 in 2002-2003 to $8,655 in 2012-2013. Alternatively, looking at the entire thirty-year period from 1982-1983 to 2012-2013 during which tax amnesty has been extensively used by the states shows that tuition and fees for in-state students at public four-year colleges and universities increased by over 257 percent (College Board 2012, Table 2A).

2. Amnesties provide citizens that have stocks of undisclosed ("black") assets accumulated through past evasion with an opportunity to declare these assets voluntarily, thereby laundering them into "white" assets (Das-Gupta and Mookherjee 1996). This implication is particularly disturbing for the United States where the underground "black" economy is growing over the years. See Tanzi (1983), and Schneider and Enste (2000).

References

Allison, Paul D. 1984. *Event History Analysis: Regression for Longitudinal Event Data* Quantitative Applications in the Social Sciences, 07–946, Newbury Park, CA: Sage Publications.

Alm, James, and William Beck. 1990. "Tax Amnesties and Tax Revenues." *Public Finance Quarterly* 18(4): 433–53.

Alm, James, and William Beck. 1991. "Wiping the Slate Clean: Individual Response to State Tax Amnesties." *Southern Economic Journal* 57(4): 1043–53.

Alm, James, and William Beck. 1993. "Tax Amnesties and Compliance in the Long Run: A Time Series Analysis." *National Tax Journal* 46(1): 53–60.

Alm, James, Jorge Martinez-Vazques, and Sally Wallace. 2000. "Tax Amnesties and Tax Collections in the Russian Federation." In *Proceedings of the 93rd Annual Conference of Taxation* 239–47. Washington D.C.: National Tax Association.

Alm, James, Michael McKee, and William Beck. 1990. "Amazing Grace: Tax Amnesties and Compliance." *National Tax Journal* 43(1): 23–37.

Alm, James. 1998. "Tax Policy Analysis: The Introduction of a Russian Tax Amnesty." Working Paper 98–6, International Studies Program, Georgia State University, October 1998.

Alm, James. 2005. "Tax Evasion." In *The Encyclopedia of Taxation and Tax Policy*, edited by Joseph J. Cordes, Robert D. Ebel, and Jane G. Gravelle, 401– 4. Washington D.C.: The Urban Institute Press.

Andreoni, James. 1991. "The Desirability of a Permanent Tax Amnesty." *Journal of Public Economics* 45(2): 143–59.

Buckwalter, Neal, Nathan Y. Sharp, Jaron H. Wilde, and David A. Wood. 2013. "Are State Tax Amnesty Programs Associated with Financial Reporting Irregularities?" SSRN Working Paper, February 2013.

Chow, Gregory C. 1960. "Test of Equality Between Sets of Coefficients in Two Linear Regressions." *Econometrica* 28(3): 591–605.

Christian, Charles W., Sanjay Gupta, and James C. Young. 2002. "Evidence on Subsequent Filing from the State of Michigan's Income Tax Amnesty." *National Tax Journal* 55(4): 703–21.

College Board. 2012. "Trends in College Pricing 2012." Trends in Higher Education Series, CollegeBoard Advocacy and Policy Center. Available at http://trends.collegeboard.org.

Commerce Clearing House, Inc., *State Tax Handbook* 1980 – 2003.

Cox, D. R., and E. J. Snell. 1968. "A General Definition of Residuals." *Journal of the Royal Statistical Society, Series B (Methodological)* 30(2): 248–75.

Cunningham, Thomas J., and Gikas A. Hardouvelis. 1992. "Money and Interest Rates: The Effects of Temporal Aggregation and Data Revisions." *Journal of Economics and Business* 44(1): 19–30.

Cuthbertson, Keith, Stephen G. Hall, and Mark P. Taylor. 1992. *Applied Econometric Techniques* London: Philip Allan.

Das-Gupta, Arindam, and Dilip Mookherjee. 1996. "Tax Amnesties as Asset Laundering Devices." *Journal of Law, Economics, & Organization* 12(2): 408–31.

Dubin, Jeffrey A., Michael J. Graetz, and Louis L. Wilde. 1992. "State Income Tax Amnesties: Causes." *The Quarterly Journal of Economics* 107(3): 1057–70.

Engle, Robert F., and Clive W. J. Granger. 1987. "Co-Integration and Error Correction: Representation, Estimation, and Testing." *Econometrica* 55(2): 251–76.

Engle, Robert F., David F. Hendry, and Jean-Francois Richard. 1983. "Exogeneity." *Econometrica* 51(2): 277–304.

Ermini, Luigi. 1989. "Some New Evidence on the Timing of Consumption Decisions and on Their Generating Process." *The Review of Economics and Statistics* 71(4): 643–50.

Federation of Tax Administrators *http://www.taxadmin.org/fta/rate/amnesty1.pdf*

Federation of Tax Administrators. 1990. "State Tax Amnesty Programs." Research Report No 133, Washington D.C.

Fisher, Ronald C., John H. Goddeeris, and James C. Young. 1989. "Participation in Tax Amnesties: The Individual Income Tax." *National Tax Journal* 42(1): 15–27.

Gino, Francesca, Don A. Moore, and Max H. Bazerman. 2008. "See No Evil: When we Overlook Other People's Unethical Behavior." Harvard Business School NOM Working Paper No. 08–045.

Granger, Clive W. J. 1990. "Aggregation of Time-Series Variables: A Survey." In *Disaggregation in Econometric Modelling,* edited by Terry Barker and M. Hashem Pesaran 17–34. London: Routledge.

Gujarati, Damodar N. 2003. *Basic Econometrics.* New York: McGraw Hill.

Halvorsen, Robert, and Raymond Palmquist. 1980. "The Interpretation of Dummy Variables in Semilogarithmic Equations." *The American Economic Review* 70(3): 474–5.

Hamilton, James D. 1994. *Time Series Analysis.* New Jersey: Princeton University Press.

Hamermesh, Daniel S. 2007. "Viewpoint: Replication in Economics." *Canadian Journal of Economics* 40(3): 715–33.

Harvey, Andrew. 1997. "Trends, Cycles and Autoregressions." *The Economic Journal* 107(440): 192–201.

Hasseldine, John. 1998. "Tax Amnesties: An International Review." *Bulletin for International Fiscal Documentation* 52(7): 303–10.

Holcombe, Randall G. 2001. "Public Choice and Public Finance." In *The Elgar Companion to Public Choice,* edited by William F. Shughart II and Laura Razzolini 396–421. Cheltenham, UK: Edward Elgar.

Holcombe, Randall G., and Russell S. Sobel. 1997. *Growth and Variability in State Tax Revenue: An Anatomy of State Fiscal Crises.* Westport, CT: Greenwood Press.

Jackson, Ira A. 1986. "Amnesty and Creative Tax Administration." *National Tax Journal* 39(3): 317–23.

Joulfaian, David. 1988. "Participation in Tax Amnesties: Evidence from a State." In *Proceedings of the Eighty-first Annual Conference on Taxation* 128–32. Washington D.C.: National Tax Association.

Kalaitzidakis, Pantelis, Theofanis P. Mamuneas, and Thanasis Stengos. 2011. "An Updated Ranking of Academic Journals in Economics." *Canadian Journal of Economics* 44(4): 1525–38.

Kennedy, Peter. 2003. *A Guide to Econometrics.* Cambridge: MIT Press.

Kiefer, Nicholas M. 1988. "Economic Duration Data and Hazard Functions." *Journal of Economic Literature* 26(2): 646–79.

Le Borgne, Eric. 2006. "Economic and Political Determinants of Tax Amnesties in the U.S. States." IMF Working Paper, WP/06/222, International Monetary Fund.

Leonard, Herman B., and Richard J. Zeckhauser. 1986. "Amnesty, Enforcement and Tax Policy." National Bureau of Economic Research, Working Paper # 2096.

Lerman, Allen H. 1986. "Tax Amnesty: The Federal Perspective." *National Tax Journal* 39(3): 325–32.

Liebowitz, S. J., and J. P. Palmer. 1984. "Assessing the Relative Impacts of Economic Journals." *Journal of Economic Literature* 22(1): 77–88.

Luitel, Hari S. 2007. "Short-run and Long-run Effects of Tax Amnesties on Tax Revenues: Evidences from US States." In *Proceedings of the Hundredth Annual Conference on Taxation* 402–13. Washington, D.C.: National Tax Association.

Luitel, Hari S. 2013. "Sensitivity of Assumptions in Duration Analysis." In *Mimeo,* Algoma University, August 2013.

Luitel, Hari S., and Mehmet S. Tosun. 2013. "A Reexamination of State Fiscal Health and Amnesty Enactment." *International Tax and Public Finance* forthcoming.

Luitel, Hari S., and Russell S. Sobel. 2007. "The Revenue Impact of Repeated Tax Amnesties." *Public Budgeting and Finance* 27(3): 19–38.

Luitel, Hari S., Gerry J. Mahar, Krishna Kadiyala, Daniel Friyia, and Brandon Mackinnon. 2014. "Are the Economies of Canada and the United States Integrated? Evidence from Cointegration Analysis." In *Mimeo,* Algoma University, May 2014.

Malik, Arun S., and Robert M. Schwab. 1991. "The Economics of Tax Amnesties." *Journal of Public Economics* 46(1): 29–49.

Marcellino, Massimiliano. 1999. "Some Consequences of Temporal Aggregation in Empirical Analysis." *Journal of Business and Economic Statistics* 17(1): 129–36.

Marè, Mauro and Carmelo Salleo. 2003. "Is One More Tax Amnesty Really That Bad? Some Empirical Evidence from the Italian 1991 VAT Amnesty." *Unpublished paper.*

Mikesell, John L. 1986. "Amnesties for State Tax Evaders: The Nature of and Response to Recent Programs." *National Tax Journal* 39(4): 507–25.

Mikesell, John L., and Justin M. Ross. 2012. "Fast Money? The Contribution of State Tax Amnesties to Public Revenue Systems." *National Tax Journal* 65(3): 529–62.

Moosa, Imad. 2011. "The Failure of Financial Econometrics: Assessing the Cointegration "Revolution"." *The Capco Institute Journal of Financial Transformation,* Applied Finance # 32. (Available at: http://www.capco.com/sites/all/files/journal-32_article-11.pdf)

National Association of State Budget Officers [NASBO]. 2004. *Budget Shortfalls: Strategies for Closing Spending and Revenue Gaps* Fourth Edition, Washington D.C.

Parle, William M., and Mike W. Hirlinger. 1986. "Evaluating the Use of Tax Amnesty by State Governments." *Public Administration Review* 46(3): 246–55.

Ross, Bonnie G. 1986. "Federal Tax Amnesty: Reflecting on the States' Experiences." *The Tax Lawyer* 40(1): 145–84.

Rossana, Robert J., and John J. Seater. 1992. "Aggregation, Unit Roots and the Time Series Structure of Manufacturing Real Wages." *International Economic Review* 33(1): 159–79.

Rossana, Robert J., and John J. Seater. 1995. "Temporal Aggregation and Economic Time Series." *Journal of Business and Economic Statistics* 13(4): 441–51.

Schneider, Friedrich, and Dominik H. Enste. 2000. "Shadow Economies: Size, Causes, and Consequences." *Journal of Economic Literature* 38: 77–114.

Stella, Peter. 1991. "An Economic Analysis of Tax Amnesties." *Journal of Public Economics* 46(3): 383–400.

Stock, James H., and Mark W. Watson. 2003. *Introduction to Econometrics.* New York: Addison Wesley.

Tanzi, Vito. 1983. "The Underground Economy in the United States: Annual Estimates, 1930–80." *Staff Papers - International Monetary Fund* 30(2): 283–305.

Torgler, Benno, and Christoph A. Schaltegger. 2005. "Tax Amnesties and Political Participation." *Public Finance Review* 33(3): 403–31.

Torgler, Benno, Christoph A. Schaltegger, and Markus Schaffner. 2003. "Is Forgiveness Divine? A Cross-Culture Comparison of Tax Amnesties." *Schweizerische Zeitschrift für Volkswirtschaft und Statistik* 139(3): 375–96.

Uchitelle, Elliot. 1989. "The Effectiveness of Tax Amnesty Programs in Selected Countries." *Federal Reserve Bank of New York Quarterly Review* 14(3): 48–53.

United States Census Bureau, *Population Estimates,* Washington, D.C.

United States Census Bureau, *State Government Finances*, Washington, D.C.

United States Census Bureau, *State Government Finances,* Washington, D.C. *Book of the State.* Various years.

United States Census Bureau, *State Government Finances,* Washington, D.C. *Statistical Abstract of the United States.* Various years.

United States Congress, Joint Committee on Taxation. 1998. Tax Amnesty (JCS-2–98). Washington, D.C.

United States Department of Commerce, Bureau of Economic Analysis, *State and Local Personal Income,* Washington, D. C.

United States Department of Labor, Bureau of Labor Statistics *Demographics* Washington, D.C.

Wei, William W. S. 1982. "The Effects of Systematic Sampling and Temporal Aggregation on Causality – A Cautionary Note." *Journal of the American Statistical Association* 77(378): 316–19.

Zellner, Arnold, and Franz Palm. 1974. "Time Series Analysis and Simultaneous Equation Econometric Models." *Journal of Econometrics* 2(1): 17–54.

Index

About the Author

Hari S. Luitel is assistant professor in the Department of Business & Economics at Algoma University. He received his PhD in economics from West Virginia University in 2005. His research interests include public economics, comparative international tax systems, fiscal policy, monetary policy, macroeconomics, and time series econometric analysis.

CPSIA information can be obtained at www.ICGtesting.com
Printed in the USA
BVOW05*1101110814

362148BV00001B/1/P